This book was very loved
But we needed room for new.
We hope you will enjoy it
Just as much as we did, too.

New Haven Free
Public Library
133 Elm St.
New Haven, CT
06510

nhfpl
NEW HAVEN FREE PUBLIC LIBRARY

D1273983

DANIEL
INOUYE

ASIAN AMERICANS OF ACHIEVEMENT

Margaret Cho

Daniel Inouye

Michelle Kwan

Bruce Lee

Maya Lin

Yo-Yo Ma

Isamu Noguchi

Amy Tan

Vera Wang

Kristi Yamaguchi

ASIAN AMERICANS
OF ACHIEVEMENT

DANIEL INOUYE

LOUISE CHIPLEY SLAVICEK

CHELSEA HOUSE
PUBLISHERS
An imprint of Infobase Publishing

Daniel Inouye

Copyright © 2007 by Infobase Publishing

Chelsea House
An imprint of Infobase Publishing
132 West 31st Street
New York, NY 10001

ISBN-10: 0-7910-9271-2
ISBN-13: 978-0-7910-9271-2

Library of Congress Cataloging-in-Publication Data
Slavicek, Louise Chipley, 1956-
  Daniel Inouye / Louise Chipley Slavicek.
    p. cm.— (Asian Americans of achievement)
Includes bibliographical references and index.
Audience: Grades 9-12.
ISBN 0-7910-9271-2 (hardcover)
  1. Inouye, Daniel K., 1924—Juvenile literature. 2. Legislators—United States—Biography—Juvenile literature. 3. United States. Congress. Senate—Biography—Juvenile literature. 4. Japanese Americans—Hawaii—Biography—Juvenile literature. 5. Asian Americans—Biography—Juvenile literature. I. Title. II. Series.
  E840.8.I5S58 2007
  328.73092—dc22
  [B]   2006026062

You can find Chelsea House on the World Wide Web at http://www.chelseahouse.com

Series design by Erika K. Arroyo
Cover design by Ben Peterson

Printed in the United States of America

Bang EJB 10 9 8 7 6 5 4 3 2 1

This book is printed on acid-free paper.

CONTENTS

December 7, 1941

On a balmy Sunday morning a few weeks before Christmas in 1941, the world as he knew it came to an abrupt end for 17-year-old Daniel Inouye. Although most Japanese Americans on the Hawaiian Island of Oahu followed the Buddhist or Shinto religions of their ancestral land, the Inouyes were Christian. As was their habit on the Sabbath, the family had risen early on December 7 to dress and enjoy a leisurely breakfast before heading to church. Danny had just clicked on the small radio that he kept near his bed and begun to button his shirt when he heard the news. In his autobiography, *Journey to Washington*, he wrote about the moment that changed his life forever.

"This is no test!" the frenzied voice of the radio announcer was yelling. "Pearl Harbor is being bombed by the Japanese! I repeat: This is not a test or a maneuver! Japanese war planes are attacking Oahu!" Danny froze in disbelief, his fingers clutching a shirt button. "It's not true!" he told himself. "It is a test, or a mistake! It can't be true!" Suddenly, he noticed his father standing in the hallway outside his bedroom, listening intently.

A small boat rescues a crew member from the battleship USS *West Virginia*, following the Japanese bombing of Pearl Harbor, Hawaii, on December 7, 1941. In just two hours, the Japanese air attack sank or severely damaged 21 American naval vessels and claimed the lives of nearly 2,400 U.S. military personnel.

Daniel would later remember that there was a sort of agony on Hyotaro Inouye's face as the announcer blared on: "This is the real thing! Pearl Harbor has been hit. . . . We can see the Japanese planes!"

Seconds later, Hyotaro Inouye and his eldest son stood in front of their Honolulu home gazing westward toward Pearl Harbor, headquarters of the U.S. Pacific Fleet. Above the harbor, black pillars of smoke billowed into the pale blue sky, shadowing the mountains that edged Oahu's western coast. Danny knew without the slightest doubt that this was no drill. Then he spotted the planes. There were three of them, zooming northward out of the thick, dirty smoke in neat military formation. As the planes soared closer, Daniel could clearly make out the red dots on their pearl-gray wingtips: the rising sun of the Japanese empire.

"You fools!" Hyotaro Inouye cried out bitterly as the warplanes droned overhead. Like the vast majority of *Issei*—Japanese immigrants to the United States—Hyotaro had worked long and hard to gain acceptance and build a stable life for himself and his family in the white-dominated and often racist society of his adopted homeland. Now, in one horrifying moment, it seemed as though all of Hyotaro's efforts were about to be undone.

In a span of just two hours, Japan's surprise attack on Pearl Harbor and nearby airfields destroyed or damaged virtually all of the 394 military aircraft on the island of Oahu; sank or crippled 21 naval vessels; and took the lives of 2,400 U.S. military personnel. Americans in the U.S. territory of Hawaii and throughout the U.S. mainland were outraged by the bloody and unprovoked assault. For them, December 7, 1941, truly was "a date which will live in infamy," as President Franklin D. Roosevelt famously called it.

Twenty-four hours after the attack, on December 8, 1941, Congress overwhelmingly approved Roosevelt's request for a declaration of war against the Japanese empire. Three days later, Congress also declared war on Japan's Axis allies, Germany and Italy. Since World War II had erupted in Europe in September 1939, the Roosevelt administration had been moving slowly but steadily toward war, even though most Americans still hoped to keep their nation out of the conflict—until the morning of December 7. By the beginning of December

With the overwhelming backing of the U.S. Congress, President Franklin D. Roosevelt signed a declaration of war against the Japanese empire on December 8, 1941, just one day after the surprise attack on Pearl Harbor. Three days later, Congress also declared war on Japan's allies, Germany and Italy.

1941, the United States was the only major global power that had managed to avoid becoming embroiled in the hostilities. In Europe, Nazi troops had overrun Poland, the Netherlands,

Belgium, Denmark, Norway, France, Greece, and Yugoslavia and had invaded the Soviet Union. In North Africa, Germans and Italians fought the British for control of the Mediterranean Sea. Half a world away, in East Asia, Japanese armies had conquered much of northern China and were pushing into French Indochina. Despite the inroads made by the Nazis and their allies as of late 1941, it was not until the Japanese raid on Oahu that a shocked American public and Congress finally resolved to put a stop to the Axis powers once and for all.

On December 9, 1941, in a radio address to the American people from the Oval Office, Roosevelt warned that the nation was embarking on what was certain to be "a long war . . . a hard war." By the time World War II finally ended in 1945, more than 400,000 American servicemen and -women were dead and another 670,000 wounded. For no other group of Americans was the war more devastating, though, than it was for those of Japanese descent.

Americans of all ethnic and racial backgrounds were filled with dread and grief during the dark weeks and months that followed the Japanese assault on Pearl Harbor, which was the first attack on U.S. territory by a foreign power since the War of 1812. For Japanese Americans such as Hyotaro and Daniel Inouye, however, anxiety and sorrow were tinged with a deep sense of shame that the bombers had come from the country of their own or their parents' birth. To make matters worse, almost immediately after the raid, ethnic Japanese residents of Hawaii and the U.S. mainland found their patriotism called into question simply because they resembled the enemy. Three months after the attack on Pearl Harbor, racial prejudice combined with wartime hysteria prompted the U.S. government to order the removal of more than 100,000 men, women, and children of Japanese ancestry—most of them U.S. citizens—from their Pacific Coast homes to isolated and heavily guarded internment camps. Their imprisonment was based not on evidence of

During World War II, Daniel Inouye was a member of the Army's all-Japanese American unit, the celebrated 442nd Regimental Combat Team. By the end of the war, the 442nd had carried the distinction of being the most highly decorated military unit of its size in U.S. history.

espionage, or treason: rather, the internees' only "crime" was their ethnic origin.

In Hawaii, where Issei and *Nisei* (the Issei's American-born children) made up more than one-third of the population and were an essential part of the Islands' workforce and economy, there was no mass internment of ethnic Japanese residents. Nonetheless, in the wake of the Pearl Harbor attack, Islanders of Japanese heritage were targets of insults, taunts, and, occasionally, fists hurled at them by hostile whites. Far more distressing to many Japanese Americans was the federal government's decision to classify all people of Japanese ancestry who lived in the United States and its territories as "4-C," or "enemy alien," meaning that they were barred from joining the armed forces. In early 1943, after a year of nonstop petitioning by Hawaiian and mainland Nisei determined to fight for their country, the government finally relented and allowed Japanese Americans to enlist in the military. Desperate not only to defend his nation but also to demonstrate loyalty to his American homeland, 18-year-old Daniel Inouye was among the very first Nisei to volunteer.

A fierce desire to prove their patriotism to their fellow Americans impelled Inouye and many of the Nisei who served in the U.S. armed forces during World War II to perform acts of extraordinary bravery and sacrifice on the battlefield. By the war's end, the entirely Japanese American 442nd Regimental Combat Team, to which Inouye belonged, had suffered enormous casualties and become the most highly decorated unit of its size in the history of the U.S. military. Inouye himself eventually received 15 medals for his wartime heroism, including the prestigious Medal of Honor. He earned this honor for continuing to lead a charge up a heavily defended enemy-held hill, even after suffering severe wounds to his abdomen and arm.

When he first spotted the Japanese planes flying over Honolulu with "pilots that looked like me," Daniel Inouye mused more than a half century later, "the world came to an end for me. I was old enough to know nothing would be the same." The high school senior was right: Neither his island home nor the American nation as a whole would ever be the same after the

Japanese attack on Oahu. What Danny could not have imagined on that long-ago December day was the critical role he would play in creating the new social and political order that emerged in Hawaii and across the United States in the wake of Pearl Harbor and World War II. During a congressional career that has already spanned more than four decades, Inouye, the first Japanese American to be elected to the U.S. House of Representatives and the U.S. Senate, has helped shape the postwar world in vital ways through his unwavering dedication to public service, international peace, and the advancement of racial equality.

2

Coming to Hawaii

One September night in 1899, in the Japanese village of Yokoyama, a fire broke out in the house of Wasaburo Inouye, Daniel Inouye's great-grandfather. No one knew exactly how the blaze started—perhaps a kerosene lamp was to blame—but before the fire could be extinguished, the Inouyes' home and two neighboring houses lay in ruins.

The next morning, the village elders met to discuss the calamity that had struck their tiny community. According to the traditional peasant culture of southern Japan, the owner of the house in which a fire began was honor-bound to pay for the rebuilding of any other houses that caught fire and for all lost belongings. After much deliberation, the elders decided that Inouye owed his neighbors the equivalent of $400.

Wasaburo was crushed. Yokoyama was a poor farming village. Like most men in the remote mountain community, once he had paid his taxes each year, he had barely enough money left to support himself and his family. Moreover, he was not a young man; most of his children were grown, and he was a

15

Workers harvest sugarcane on a plantation on central Oahu, Hawaii, in this early twentieth century photo. During the early 1900s, life was difficult for sugar plantation laborers like Daniel Inouye's grandparents. Typically, they toiled 10 to 12 hours a day, six days a week, under a blistering sun.

grandfather many times over. He could never hope to raise $400, no matter how hard or long he toiled. There was only one way to pay off the debt and preserve the family's honor, Wasaburo decided. He would have to send his eldest son, Asakichi, far away from the only home he had ever known. Asakichi must go to Hawaii, where, it was said, a man could earn good money laboring on the vast sugar plantations.

The cultivation of sugarcane had been a vital part of the Hawaiian economy since 1835, when three enterprising Americans established the archipelago's first permanent sugar plantation on the island of Kauai. The island chain's subtropical climate was ideally suited to growing sugarcane, and in no time Hawaii's new industry was booming. The chiefly American-born owners of the profitable new sugar plantations had a problem, however: Hawaii could not provide enough workers to harvest the ever-expanding crops. When Captain James Cook of the British navy first "discovered" the remote archipelago in 1778, Hawaii's eight major islands were home to an estimated 300,000 people, descendants of Polynesians who had sailed there from other Pacific islands centuries earlier. By the mid-1800s, however, diseases such as smallpox and measles had killed off much of Hawaii's native population. These diseases were brought to the once-isolated archipelago by traders, whalers, and missionaries who arrived after Cook's "discovery." In 1853, just 73,000 native Hawaiians were left on the island chain; 20 years later, that number had fallen to 57,000.

By the 1850s, the sugar planters concluded that they had no choice but to bring in foreign workers. They had heard that Asians were generally willing to work longer hours for lower wages than European or American laborers. Plantation recruiters naturally focused their efforts on the two most populous countries in the region, China and Japan. Traditionally suspicious of outsiders, the Japanese government had long discouraged immigration to foreign lands; for many years, therefore, China remained Hawaii's chief source for Asian labor. During the 1880s, however, Japan suffered a severe economic downturn. Many people, particularly in the country's crowded south, desperately needed work. Emperor Meiji, Japan's ruler, worried that his nation's economic troubles might lead to mass unrest and even a revolution. When the Hawaiian sugar barons promised good wages and free housing to any Japanese willing to undertake the nearly 4,000-mile voyage to the archipelago, Emperor Meiji listened. In 1884, he proclaimed that his subjects could seek employment on the island kingdom and the flood-gates of Japanese immigration to Hawaii were opened.

In the 10 years that followed Emperor Meiji's proclamation, thousands of peasants and manual laborers signed labor contracts with the Hawaiian recruiters who visited Japan's cities and villages to look for workers. The number of Japanese who left their homeland to work in Hawaii's cane fields grew even more rapidly after 1898, when Hawaii was annexed by the United States and America's Chinese Exclusion Act went into effect on the archipelago. The Exclusion Act was passed in 1882 at the urging of whites who were fearful that the growing number of Chinese migrants willing to work for low pay would depress wages for all Americans. It slammed the door on further Chinese immigration to the United States. Barred from importing Chinese workers, Hawaii's sugar planters stepped up their recruiting efforts in Japan. Just two years after annexation, the number of Japanese living in Hawaii had more than doubled from 25,000 to approximately 61,000.

By late 1899, when Wasaburo Inouye decided to send his son to the Islands, Japanese workers made up 70 percent of the Hawaiian sugar industry's labor force. Few of these Japanese-born laborers thought of Hawaii as home, however. The majority viewed themselves as *dekaseginin,* a Japanese term that means "workers away from home." Dekaseginin did not intend to stay in Hawaii permanently; their goal was to return to Japan as soon as they had earned enough money to purchase a few acres of farmland back home or to pay off their debts. Most hoped to be back in their native land within three to five years—the typical length of the labor contracts that they signed with the sugar companies.

Like most of his Japanese compatriots, Asakichi Inouye had a powerful sense of belonging to his ancestral land. The thought of leaving his lifelong home filled the 28-year-old with sadness and apprehension. Hawaii and its people were completely unknown to him; not a single soul from Yokoyama had ever been to the faraway archipelago. There was no telling what hardships he might encounter there; nor was there any way to know how long it would take him to earn the $400 he needed before he could return home.

As much as Asakichi longed to remain in Yokoyama, he knew that he must do his father's bidding. Obedience and respect toward parents was a central element of Japanese culture. According to Japanese religious and ethical teachings, every person owed a tremendous debt to his or her parents for giving him or her the gift of life. Even for a grown child such as Asakichi, failure to comply with a father's request was considered deeply shameful.

Before setting off on the 100-mile journey to Fukuoka City to meet with the sugar company recruiters, Asakichi got up the nerve to ask his father for one important favor. He wanted his wife, Moyo, and their only son, four-year-old Hyotaro, to come with him to Hawaii. Wasaburo was torn; he had assumed that Moyo, Hyotaro, and Moyo and Asakichi's two young daughters would reside with him in Yokoyama. Asakichi would not be able to pay off the debt as quickly if he had to support a child and spouse in Hawaii. In the end, though, Wasaburo could not bring himself to deny his son's request. "Very well," he sighed. "Take them. Let them be a reminder that you will come back to us."

In Fukuoka City, Asakichi Inouye signed a contract with a recruiting agent, agreeing to work on a Hawaiian sugar plantation for five years. In return, Asakichi was promised 10 dollars per month, free housing, and passage to the Islands for himself and his family. Asakichi, Moyo, and Hyotaro spent two miserable weeks on the sailing ship *Peking Maru* crammed into the vessel's musty steerage section with hundreds of other dekaseginin. "We were packed into the ship in one big room. There was no privacy, no comforts, no nothing. We were like silkworms on a tray, eating and sleeping," a Japanese steerage passenger remembered vividly decades later.

Finally, 15 long days after leaving their homeland, the Inouyes arrived in Hawaii's chief city and port, Honolulu. The family had scarcely disembarked when they found themselves on yet another sailing vessel, this one bound for Kauai, the most northerly of the eight main islands in the Hawaiian Archipelago and home to Asakichi's new employer, the McBryde Sugar Plantation.

Life had never been easy for the Inouyes: Despite toiling long hours in his father's rice paddies and tea fields, Asakichi had struggled to earn enough to feed and clothe his family back in Yokoyama. Still, nothing either Asakichi or Moyo had ever experienced could prepare them for the appalling housing and working conditions they encountered at the McBryde Plantation. On arriving at the 5,000-acre farm, the family headed straight to Camp Two, one of several compounds on the plantation devoted to housing dekaseginin. Like most Hawaiian sugar plantations of the era, the McBryde establishment separated its workers by race and nationality; eventually, the plantation included separate camps for workers of Filipino, Puerto Rican, and Portuguese, as well as Japanese, descent. Also in common with other Hawaiian plantation owners of the time, the owners of the McBryde Plantation did not believe in pampering their employees. To their dismay, the Inouyes discovered that their new home in Camp Two was a tiny, unpainted wooden shack. As primitive as the boxlike structure was, however, it was better than the crowded barracks that the single men who formed most of the plantation's workforce were forced to live in.

At 6:00 A.M. every morning of the week except Sunday, shrill whistles called the McBryde workforce to the cane fields. There, the workers labored for 10 to 14 hours a day, often in stifling humidity. From dawn to dusk, they slaved away, plowing, planting, fertilizing, and hoeing. The fieldworkers dreaded harvest time the most. Cutting down the 12- to 14-foot (3.7- to 4.3-

The island of Kauai is known as the "garden isle" because of its lush vegetation and fertile soil. Its chief crops are sugarcane and pineapple.

meter) stalks with machetes and loading the heavy canes onto wagons or railroad cars for transport to the sugar mill was a particularly burdensome and exhausting job. No matter how hot the sun or how difficult the task, the field hands were expected to maintain a relentless work pace. Those who failed to keep up risked a fine or even a whipping from the *lunas*, the plantations' typically white—or *haole*, as native Hawaiians called Caucasians—overseers. Years later, according to the book *Whispered Silences*, a Japanese immigrant who worked in the cane fields of nearby Lihue Plantation about the time that Asakichi worked on the McBryde Plantation, recalled, "We had no time to rest. We worked like machines." Re-garding the pace of the work, another dekaseginin complained,

It burns us up to have an ignorant luna stand around and holler and swear at us all the time for not working fast enough. Every so often, just to show how good he is, he'll come up and grab a hoe and work like hell for about two minutes. . . . He knows and we know he couldn't work for ten minutes at that pace.

As it did for most of their fellow dekaseginin, the promise of high wages brought the Inouyes to Hawaii's sugarcane fields in the first place. Because Asakichi and Moyo were committed to paying off the family debt as quickly as possible, they endured the backbreaking labor and dismal housing that came with their new life on Kauai without complaint. Saving money from Asakichi's monthly pay turned out to be harder than the Inouyes had anticipated, however. Like other Hawaiian plantations, the McBryde Plantation operated its own general store where workers were forced to purchase most of their necessities. After Hawaii's annexation by the United States in 1898, company-run stores were supposed to sell goods to plantation laborers at cost. Few did. In fact, the prices charged by the stores for their merchandise were often grossly inflated. As a supposed courtesy to their customers, most stores made it easy for workers to buy what they needed on credit—yet the company-run stores were not doing their patrons any favors. At the end of each pay cycle, many workers found themselves penniless once the money they owed the store for that month's purchases had been deducted from their wages. Some McBryde employees fell so far behind in meeting their store payments that they were forced to accept second and even third five-year labor contracts.

Asakichi and Moyo lived as frugally as possible. Still, after paying off their debt to the company store at the end of each month, they were doing well if they had one dollar left to send back to Japan. At that rate, it would take a lifetime to erase the family debt and restore honor to the Inouye name. Then Asakichi had an idea. Everyone he knew in Camp Two complained about the lack of a bathhouse. Shinto, Japan's native religion, places great emphasis on cleanliness, and bathing has been an essential component of Japanese culture for centuries. Back in Japan, most people made regular visits to communal bathhouses, where they soaked in a deep, heated tub called a *furo*. Asakichi decided to build a furo in the plantation camp and charge his fellow dekaseginin a penny a bath.

Soon, Asakichi had fashioned a large, square furo using wood scavenged from the plantation grounds. Every day when his work in the fields was over, he would rush back to camp to heat the water for the tub. Asakichi knew that the lines for the furo would form quickly; soaking in its luxurious warmth felt heavenly after 12 hours of hard labor in the cane fields. In order to serve as many customers as possible, Asakichi allowed each bather exactly five minutes before he or she had to turn over the furo to the next person in line.

Not long after Asakichi built his furo, Moyo came up with another scheme designed to help them pay off the family debt sooner: selling homemade tofu cakes to the other dekaseginin. Made from curdled soybean milk, tofu has been a staple of Japanese cuisine for more than 2,000 years. Six days a week, Moyo and Asakichi rose at 2:00 A.M. to ensure that the soft white cakes would be baked and ready to sell to the workers before they headed off to the fields. Eager for any reminder of home, the residents of Camp Two snapped up Moyo's tofu, and the coins finally began to accumulate in the Inouyes' money jar.

Despite their new money-making ventures, by the time Asakichi's five-year contract with the McBryde Plantation expired in late 1904, the couple had managed to pay off only $100 of the family debt. Asakichi felt that he had no choice but to sign a second contract with the plantation's owners.

By this time, Asakichi and Moyo had reconciled themselves to the idea that they would probably have to remain in Hawaii long after Asakichi's second five-year labor contract had expired. The couple had already begun to put money aside to pay for their daughters' passage from Japan to Kauai. Asakichi also agreed to nine-year-old Hyotaro's request to attend the public grammar school in the nearby town of Eleele. At Eleele, all classes were taught in English. Learning the language of Hawaii's most powerful citizens—the men of American descent who dominated the Islands' sugar industry—could be a great advantage to Hyotaro in the future. Asakichi realized that a Japanese person who knew how to speak and read English could hope to leave the cane fields for a better life in town, perhaps as a clerk for a shipping company or as a shopkeeper.

Hyotaro's schooling progressed very slowly. By the time he reached adolescence, he was spending more days in the fields

HAWAII BECOMES A U.S. TERRITORY

By the late nineteenth century, sugar plantations had become the heart of the Hawaiian economy. As a result, the sugar planters, the vast majority of whom were either American born or of American descent, held enormous power on the Hawaiian Islands. When the independent-minded Queen Liliuokalani inherited the Hawaiian throne from her brother King Kalakaua in 1891, however, the sugar producers worried that their long-standing influence in the Islands' government could be endangered. They were also deeply concerned about promoting closer commercial ties to the United States, which had served as the chief market for Hawaiian sugar for several decades. Above all, the sugar planters hoped that the duty-free entry rights to the U.S. market that they had first obtained in 1875 could be made permanent. This was a lucrative special privilege that was being threatened in the early 1890s by new U.S. tariff laws designed to favor American sugar producers.

In 1893, the increasingly anxious sugar interests in Hawaii decided to take matters into their own hands. With the assistance with his father than in the classroom. Finally, at an age when most people graduate from high school, Hyotaro was ready to begin his secondary education. Because Kauai provided few educational opportunities for nonwhites, Hyotaro convinced his father to let him travel to Honolulu, on the island of Oahu, to attend Mills High School, a boarding school for Asians and native Hawaiians that was operated by American missionaries. Hyotaro used the money he had saved from working in the cane fields to pay for his tuition.

In keeping with the Mills school's religious orientation, all students were required to attend church services each Sunday. By his third year at Mills, Hyotaro had decided to abandon the

of other American businessmen in the Islands, they engineered a scheme to overthrow Queen Liliuokalani. Their essentially bloodless coup was over almost before it had begun, and Hawaii's monarchy was promptly dissolved. The following year, the Republic of Hawaii was established, with Sanford B. Dole, the wealthy descendant of American missionaries, as its first president. The Islands' new haole leadership began to work toward Hawaiian annexation to the United States almost immediately after the coup. Economic motives played a central role in the annexation campaign: The only way to secure exemption from American tariffs once and for all, the Islands' sugar interests reasoned, was for Hawaii to become a U.S. possession. Not until imperialist William McKinley became president of the United States in 1897, however, was the government willing to seriously consider annexing the far-off Pacific islands. McKinley successfully maneuvered a treaty of annexation through the U.S. Senate, and, on August 12, 1898, Hawaii became a U.S. possession. In 1900, Hawaii's territorial status was formally outlined and Sanford Dole was appointed as the Islands' first territorial governor.

This photograph shows a Japanese store in Honolulu, Hawaii, in 1910. By the early twentieth century, Honolulu boasted a large and vibrant Japanese community. Daniel Inouye's parents both moved to the port city as teenagers and were married in Honolulu's River Street Methodist Church in 1923.

Buddhist and Shinto faiths of his ancestors in favor of Christianity. He joined the River Street Methodist Church, which had a predominantly Japanese American congregation. At the River Street church, Hyotaro met his future wife. She was a bright and outspoken young woman by the name of Kame Imanaga.

Kame's father had also immigrated to Hawaii from Japan to work on a sugar plantation, but Kame's upbringing had been very different from Hyotaro's. Born on the island of Maui in 1902, Kame was orphaned at an early age. Her mother died soon after her birth, and her father passed away when she was just 10 years old. At first, Japanese neighbors on the plantation took turns caring for her. Then, a few months after her father's death, a native Hawaiian couple who had heard of her plight offered to take the child into their home. Kame spent several years living with the impoverished but tenderhearted Hawaiian couple, a time that she later remembered as among the happiest periods in her life. "She was never to forget the abiding kindness of the people who cared for in those troubled years," Daniel Inouye noted decades later in his autobiography, "and held ever after a special regard for the Hawaiian people."

When she was 14, a Protestant minister arranged for Kame to be sent to the Susannah Wesley Home, a church-operated orphanage in Honolulu. About a week after she arrived on Oahu, a local haole clergyman by the name of Daniel Kleinfelter visited the home on an official inspection. As he toured the institution, Kleinfelter handed a piece of candy to each child he met. All of the orphans were delighted with this rare treat, with the exception of one petite Asian girl: Kame Imanaga. Kame declined the gift, explaining that sweets meant nothing to her. The only thing she wanted was a family of her own, she declared boldly. Kleinfelter was so impressed by the outspoken teenager that he promptly invited Kame to live with him, his wife, and their two daughters in their Honolulu home.

Encouraged by her new haole family, Kame Imanaga converted to Christianity and began to attend River Street Methodist Church. Six years after her adoption, a handsome young man—Hyotaro Inouye—caught her eye at a church social. A year later, Kame and Hyotaro became husband and wife at the very church where they had first met. Having finally obtained his high school diploma, Hyotaro now worked as a file clerk with a Honolulu shipping agent. The job did not pay well, and the newlyweds moved into a cramped two-family house in one of the city's poorest Asian ghettos.

Almost exactly 12 months after their wedding, on September 7, 1924, Kame and Hyotaro became the proud parents of a baby boy. Naming the newborn was a joint project for the couple. Daniel, his first name, was Western, chosen by Kame in honor of her adoptive father, Daniel Kleinfelter. His middle name, Ken, was firmly grounded in the language and customs of the East. *Ken* is the Japanese word for "to build," and Hyotaro, the eldest son of eldest sons for four generations—a notable distinction for any traditional Japanese male—selected the name in the hope that his firstborn would continue to build the Inouye family by someday fathering a son of his own. The naming of young Daniel Ken Inouye in 1924 reflected the blending of East and West—of Japanese and American culture, beliefs, and values—that was to be a central facet of the future senator's entire upbringing.

3

Becoming American

One of Daniel Inouye's earliest memories is of a big celebration in his parents' home that took place shortly before his fifth birthday. There was much laughter and singing, and the sake, a sweet Japanese wine made from fermented rice, flowed freely. The last payment on the $400 debt incurred by his great-grandparents so many years before had finally been made. Asakichi and Moyo Inouye, newly retired from the McBryde Sugar Plantation, were jubilant. After nearly three decades of grinding labor and financial sacrifice, the honor of the Inouye clan had at last been redeemed.

The fulfillment of the family debt meant that Asakichi and Moyo could return to their native village of Yokoyama with their heads held high. Much had changed since 1899, when the couple and their young son departed Japan for far-off Hawaii, however. For one thing, Asakichi and Moyo's parents—including the family patriarch, Wasaburo—were long dead. For another, Hyotaro and his siblings were now young adults with minds of their own, and none of them had the slightest interest in moving back to Japan. They considered themselves not transplanted Japanese but Americans—and Hawaii their true home. With memories of their lives in Japan growing ever dimmer, Asakichi and Moyo realized that, at some point along the way, they, too, had begun to think of Hawaii as home. In 1929, in a letter to his younger brother Yahei in Yokoyama, Asakichi explained the couple's decision to remain in Hawaii: "My children are here, and my grandson, and it is here that I have passed most of the days of my life. I do not believe that my wife and I, in our last years, could find contentment in Yokoyama, which has become for us a strange place."

Asakichi and Moyo Inouye's gradual acceptance of Hawaii as their new homeland was hardly unique: It mirrored the experiences of tens of thousands of other Japanese who journeyed to Hawaii during the late nineteenth and early twentieth centuries intending to work on the sugar plantations for a few years and then return to Japan to enjoy the fruits of their labor. Nearly half of the approximately 200,000 dekaseginin who came to Hawaii between 1884 (when Emperor Meiji first approved the large-scale emigration of Japanese workers) and 1924 (when Congress prohibited further Japanese immigration to the United States) decided to stay permanently in the Islands. Over the years, as they had married and raised children, the migrants had put down strong new roots in the archipelago. Many dekaseginin watched their Hawaiian-born children grow up as American citizens, attend American public schools and embrace American ideals; more and more of them "realized that they had become settlers and Hawaii had become their home," noted historian Ronald Takaki in *A Different Mirror*.

The rising number of Japanese who sailed to Hawaii and the western United States during the last decades of the 1800s combined with the migrants' tendency to plant deep roots in their adopted country caused the Japanese-American population to soar. By 1900, shortly after Hawaii's annexation by the United States, people of Japanese descent made up nearly 40 percent

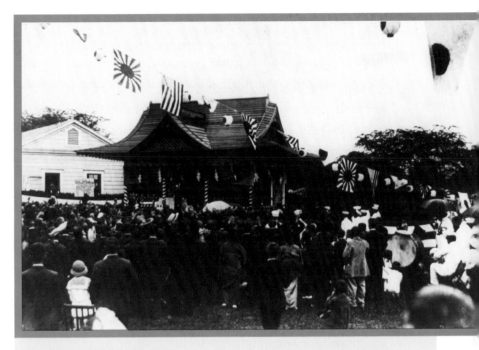

A large gathering of Japanese Hawaiians celebrate the birthday of the Japanese emperor on November 3, 1916, in Honolulu. Shortly after Hawaii officially became a territory of the United States, people of Japanese heritage made up almost 40 percent of the Islands' population.

of the Islands' population, outnumbering all of Hawaii's other ethnic and racial groups, including the Chinese, Caucasians, and native Hawaiians. Japanese immigrants made up a much smaller portion of the overall population on the U.S. mainland, but, by 1910, more than 70,000 resided in California and elsewhere on the Pacific Coast.

Some Americans were deeply uneasy about the growing Japanese population. Just as they had worried about cheap Chinese labor flooding the nation after the Civil War, labor leaders now worried that the Japanese migrants' willingness to toil long hours for modest pay would lead to lower wages and longer working days for white Americans. In Hawaii, the powerful haole leadership was also concerned about the growing

Japanese presence in their backyard. For decades, Caucasians had dominated the island chain's cultural standards as well as its political and economic life. Now, some members of Hawaii's white elite feared that the soaring Japanese population would undercut their influence in the archipelago. Soon, the haole

Being Asian American

DANIEL INOUYE AND HIS JAPANESE HERITAGE

Throughout his life and political career, Daniel Inouye has been strongly influenced by a traditional Japanese code of ethics. He first learned this code from his Japanese-born father and grandparents, and it was reinforced by his Issei instructors at the Japanese languages schools he attended during much of his childhood. Among the key elements of this code of moral behavior were a deep sense of obligation and honor (*on*) and a belief in the value of interpersonal harmony and compromise.

The traditional Japanese concept of *on*—that when an individual receives a significant gift or favor he or she is honor bound to repay the giver—was drilled into Daniel Inouye from an early age. The continuing importance of this core Japanese value for Inouye is evident in his published writings and speeches. Over the years, Inouye has related the story of his father's wartime farewell message to him regarding *on* over and over again in essays, interviews, and public addresses, as well as in his 1967 autobiography, *Journey to Washington*. The United States had given jobs and an education to the Inouyes, Hyotaro told Daniel in 1943 when he was about to depart for basic training camp on the mainland, and now *on* required that the family's great debt to America be repaid. The teenager immediately understood what his father was trying to say: Giving his all in battle—even if it meant making the ultimate sacrifice for his country—was Daniel's sacred duty. To do anything less would bring dishonor to his American homeland, his Japanese heritage, and his family.

leaders warned, the Japanese would overwhelm every other group in the Islands and Hawaii would become little more than a satellite of the Japanese empire.

In 1908, in response to pressure from anti-Japanese agitators, President Theodore Roosevelt persuaded the Japanese

Throughout the bloody campaigns he fought in France and Italy during World War II, the age-old Japanese concept of *on* was never far from his mind and helped him perform the extraordinary acts of courage for which he eventually earned 15 medals, including the Congressional Medal of Honor.

Another aspect of his ethnic heritage that has significantly shaped Daniel Inouye's attitudes and actions over the years is the traditional Japanese emphasis on interpersonal harmony and cooperation. Throughout his long congressional career, Inouye has gained a reputation for consistently promoting conciliation and compromise over confrontation. Senator Inouye is a firm believer in the importance of *otagai*, a Japanese concept that emphasizes the importance of working together effectively and fulfilling one's personal obligations to others in a group or organization. Inouye's deep respect for the principle of otagai—as well as his strong sense of bipartisanship—are particularly evident in the close working relationship he has developed with the longtime Republican senator from Alaska, Ted Stevens, who has served on the Defense Subcommittee of the Senate Appropriations Committee and the Commerce Committee with Inouye for many years. In 2001, for example, Inouye refused to cast what would have been the tie-breaking vote in support of a Democratic amendment to President Bush's tax bill because Stevens had been called away from Washington and Inouye had promised the senator that he would "pair" his votes with him that day.

government to sign a restrictive "Gentleman's Agreement" that all but sealed off the United States and its territories to Japanese laborers. The agreement did not bar the Japanese wives of men who were already working in the United States from coming to America, however. Consequently, thousands of Japanese women immigrated to Hawaii and the West Coast during the decade after the Gentleman's Agreement was finalized. The majority of them were "picture brides." Picture brides, who typically came from poor but respectable families, exchanged photographs with prospective Japanese-born husbands residing in Hawaii or on the mainland. Marriages were then arranged by the brides' and the grooms' families back in Japan. Before journeying across the Pacific, the picture brides had their names entered in the family registries of the absent grooms, which, according to Japanese custom, formalized the couple's union.

The number of picture brides who entered the United States soared after 1908, and more and more children of Japanese descent were born on American soil. As a result, anti-Japanese sentiment only deepened, particularly on the mainland. Inflammatory newspaper editorials cautioned white Americans that Asian immigrants endangered not only their wages but also American civilization itself. This increased racial hostility toward the Japanese. Racial "experts" such as sociologist Lothrop Stoddard added to the anti-Japanese feeling that swept the nation. In 1920, Stoddard published a widely read book titled *The Rising Tide of Color Against White World-Supremacy*, in which he argued forcefully against Asian immigration. Claiming that Eastern religious and political ideals were not compatible with traditional American values, Stoddard warned that the United States' booming Japanese population posed a grave threat to the American way of life.

In 1924, the same year that Daniel Inouye was born, Congress passed a restrictive new immigration law that reflected the anti-Asian ideas of Stoddard and other popular "racial theorists" of the era. The Johnson-Reed Act of 1924, the United

This photo of an early twentieth century Japanese ghetto in Honolulu shows the impoverished conditions under which many people of Japanese descent were forced to live during the time of Daniel Inouye's childhood. Ethnic Japanese residents of Hawaii—and of the U.S. mainland—confronted widespread racial discrimination in employment, housing, and even in recreational activities.

States' first complete set of immigration regulations, reduced the number of Asians allowed to enter the United States to a trickle and cut off Japanese immigration entirely.

During the 1920s and 1930s, when Daniel Inouye was growing up, people of Japanese descent in Hawaii—as on the U.S. mainland—faced widespread racial discrimination in housing, education, employment, and even in dining and other recreational activities. Typically, Japanese Americans lived in segregated communities like the Asian ghettos of Honolulu where Danny spent his childhood. They attended segregated schools and were shut out of all but the most menial and lowest-paying jobs. "You can't go very high up and get big money unless your skin is white," complained one Japanese plantation worker in *A Different Mirror.* "You can work here all your life and yet a haole who doesn't know a thing about the work can be ahead of you in no time." During much of Daniel's childhood, Hyotaro Inouye was forced to hold down two jobs to provide his family with the basic necessities. Hyotaro spent his days as a file clerk for a shipping company. In the evenings, he waited tables at the Halekulani Hotel, a Waikiki resort that catered to haole tourists from the mainland.

Despite Hyotaro's long workdays, he and Kame constantly scrimped just to make ends meet. Leftovers were unheard of in the Inouye household: Daniel later recalled that he and his three younger siblings always left the table feeling a little hungry. Kame became an expert at stretching the household's meager food budget. Each morning, she would painstakingly slice a single hard-boiled egg into six equal slices so that everyone could have a bit of protein with breakfast. Kame also kept an iron grip on the family's clothing budget. To save money, Danny usually went barefoot. Shoes, which were reserved for church, were purchased two sizes too big, and their toes were stuffed with newspaper to make them fit. No one in the family had much of a wardrobe, and wearing hand-me-downs was a way of life for the younger Inouyes. "Among all six of us," Daniel wrote in his autobiography, "we had not enough clothes to fill a closet—which worked out very nicely since none of the places where we lived had a closet!"

The fact that his family was poor did not impair Daniel's childhood, however. "I never felt deprived or sorry for myself," he later recalled. The close-knit Inouye clan went on picnics in the mountains, gathered around the upright piano that dominated the home's living room for family music nights, and designed and built an elaborate tree house in nearby woods. There, Danny and his younger sisters and brother spent many happy hours pretending to fight off villainous poachers or blood-

One of young Daniel Inouye's first jobs was working as a beach boy or surfing guide for the mainland tourists who flocked to Honolulu's most popular beach, Waikiki. Although the job didn't pay well, it allowed him to indulge in two of his favorite pastimes: surfing and swimming.

thirsty lions, just like Tarzan, their favorite fictional character, did in the jungles of Africa. "My sorrows were few and momentary and my most vivid memories are of the fun we had," Daniel wrote of his boyhood decades later. "We enjoyed each other."

Many of Daniel Inouye's most cherished boyhood memories revolve around his numerous hobbies. Danny was an enthusiastic collector of postage stamps, tropical fish, crystal radio set parts—which he eventually used to construct his own radio receiver—and, above all, homing pigeons. These are special pigeons that have been selectively bred to find their way back to their home loft. During World Wars I and II, homing pigeons were successfully used by the U.S. Signal Corps to carry messages over long distances. Daniel obtained many of the pigeons in his collection from the Army Signal Center at nearby Schofield Barracks. Daniel cleaned the center's coops, and in return the soldiers would give him a few pigeon eggs to take back to his loft. Nothing quite compared to the thrill of watching the downy yellow chicks slowly peck their way out of their shells, Daniel later recalled.

Because cash was always in short supply in the Inouye household, Danny knew better than to ask his parents to help fund his numerous hobbies. To pay for his beloved pastimes, he took on an assortment of odd jobs such as babysitting, mowing lawns, and trimming his friends' hair. When Daniel was old enough to drive, he also earned a few dollars parking cars at Honolulu Stadium during baseball games. His favorite job of all, however, was that of "beach boy."

Throughout Daniel's growing-up years, the Inouyes never lived far from the ocean. Daniel quickly became adept at spear fishing, swimming, and Hawaii's famous native sport, surfing. When Danny was in his early teens, he began to hire himself out on weekends as a beach boy—or surfing guide—for the tourists who crowded Waikiki, Honolulu's best beach. First, Danny would guide the novice surfer out to where the waves were starting to form. Then he would teach his client how to stand on the flat board without losing his or her balance—a difficult undertaking for most beginners. When a big wave caught the surfboard, Danny would shove his customer off on an exhilarating ride back to the beach. Daniel faced plenty of competition from the dozens of other beach boys—most of them native Hawaiians—who gathered each afternoon near Waikiki's hotels, so he had no choice but to keep his fees low. Nevertheless, he loved the work. Beach boys were expected to retrieve a client's surfboard from the breakers if the tourist happened to fall off—a common occurrence—but Daniel did not mind this aspect of the job, viewing it merely as an opportunity for a refreshing swim.

East and West

Throughout Daniel's childhood and teenage years, life in the Inouye household was a harmonious mix of Japanese and American customs and ideals. "There were no jangling conflicts between East and West in our house, but a kind of stimulating blend of the two that characterized the entire Japanese community in Hawaii," Inouye recalled. When they ate roast beef, the family used forks and knives at the dinner table. When they ate traditional Japanese dishes like sukiyaki or tempura, they used chopsticks. Daniel's parents emphasized Japanese values such as respect for elders and the importance of upholding the family's honor. They also taught their children to believe in the "American dream": that, in America, a brighter future awaited any person who was willing to work hard and persevere. As Kame Inouye often told her children, "I take from the old ways what I think is good and useful. I take from the new ways what is good and useful. Anyone would be foolish not to."

Like most Japanese-American children during the 1920s and 1930s, Daniel spent hours each afternoon studying the language and customs of his ancestors at a private Japanese school. His parents never allowed Danny's Japanese education to interfere with his American education, however. In fact, Kame and Hyotaro made a major personal sacrifice in the hope of helping Daniel succeed in the American-run public schools he attended from kindergarten through twelfth grade. A few months before Danny headed off to kindergarten for the first time, his parents abruptly switched from speaking only Japanese at home to speaking only English. Carrying on conversations in English was especially challenging for Kame. Like most Asian Hawaiians of her era, she had never learned to speak "proper," or standard, English. Instead, she spoke what was popularly known as pidgin, a hybrid form of English that was peppered with words from other languages. "Depending on her mood and what she wanted to say," Daniel later remembered, Kame would add a generous smattering of Japanese, Chinese, Hawaiian, and even Portuguese words to her particular version of pidgin. (It is not surprising that a number of Portuguese words found their way into Kame's speech. Many Portuguese settled in Hawaii during the late nineteenth and early twentieth centuries.)

Kame and Hyotaro's insistence on speaking only English at home once Daniel started his American education was closely linked to their belief that they and their children were first and foremost Americans and that the United States, not Japan, was the country to which the family owed its primary allegiance. Because they had been born in the U.S. territory of Hawaii, Daniel and his three siblings were all U.S. citizens. Despite Hyotaro and Kame's devotion to the United States, neither of them was a citizen—and they did not have any hope of ever becoming citizens under existing laws. In 1790, soon after the founding of the American Republic, Congress passed a naturalization act that barred all nonwhite immigrants to the country from becoming citizens. That legislation was changed shortly after the Civil

War ended in 1865 so that the newly freed slaves—as well as any African-born immigrant to the United States—could apply for citizenship. The revised naturalization rules did not affect the status of Asian-born immigrants, however; they remained "aliens ineligible to citizenship" under federal law. In 1907, Congress passed a new immigration act that had the effect of further restricting citizenship for Japanese and other Asians who lived in the United States. According to the Expatriation Act of that year, any U.S.-born woman who married an alien automatically forfeited her American citizenship. Kame Imanaga was born on the island of Maui two years after Hawaii became a U.S. territory. When she married Japanese native Hyotaro Inouye, she automatically lost her status as an American citizen and became an "alien ineligible to citizenship," just like her new husband.

Although he was fiercely loyal to his adopted land, Hyotaro Inouye wanted his children to know and respect his birth country's rich culture and history. He insisted that Daniel and his siblings attend a private Japanese language school every day after their public school classes were finished. All of the school's instructors revered the ancient customs and wisdom of their ancestral land and encouraged their young American-born students to take pride in their Japanese heritage. One instructor, an elderly Buddhist priest who specialized in Japanese ethics and history, carried his devotion to the old country and its ways much further. He tried to persuade his pupils that Japanese culture was superior to all other cultures and that the children's primary loyalty ought to be to the land of their ancestors and not to the United States. This contradicted everything Daniel had been taught both at home and in public school and left him feeling uneasy, particularly when relations between the governments of the United States and Japan began to sour during the late 1930s.

By the end of the 1930s, there had been signs of impending trouble between Japan and the United States for some time.

Over the course of the previous three decades, the two nations had gradually emerged as the Pacific region's leading naval and commercial powers. As they steadily expanded their military and economic influence in the Pacific during the early twentieth century, they also came to view one another as untrustworthy and potentially dangerous. Japan's leaders resented the United States for its racist immigration policies, especially after the passage of the Johnson-Reed Act of 1924. American leaders were alarmed by Japan's growing imperialist ambitions in the Far East. In 1931, Japan's ultranationalistic rulers had embarked on a brutal campaign of expansion in the weak and divided Republic of China. After turning the province of Manchuria into a Japanese puppet state, in 1937, they launched a full-scale invasion of China that came to be known as the Second Sino-Japanese War. Japan's new war of aggression in China disturbed the American leadership and also created much ill feeling toward the Japanese empire among Americans in general. Most people in Hawaii, as on the U.S. mainland, sympathized openly with the Chinese, who suffered enormous casualties during the conflict. Many Japanese Hawaiians, especially the American-born Nisei, felt deeply shamed by their ancestral land's unprovoked attack on China and particularly by the Japanese air force's attacks on civilian targets. In the days before television, newsreels—short news films that covered national and world events—were typically played in movie theaters prior to the feature film. According to a report in a Hawaiian Japanese-language newspaper, young Nisei at a local theater looked "miserable after watching newsreel pictures of Japanese planes bombing Chinese cities."

Just as Japan's imperialistic and bloody campaign in China was drawing increasing criticism from the U.S. government and the public, Daniel's Japanese ethics and history teacher was becoming more pro-Japanese and anti-American in his classroom lectures. Week after week, the old priest hammered away at the foolishness of the American government in opposing what

Japanese troops invaded Manchuria in 1931 and soon established a puppet state in the northern Chinese province. Six years later the expansionist Japanese empire launched a full-scale invasion of China. Japan's bloody war of aggression against China generated resentment toward the empire among many Americans and made many people of Japanese descent living in Hawaii and on the U.S. mainland during the 1930s deeply uncomfortable.

he viewed as Japan's "grand destiny": expanding its influence throughout China and all of East Asia. His teacher's disgust with the U.S. leadership deepened during the summer of 1939: Hoping to pressure Japan into withdrawing from China, Congress refused to renew a 30-year-old commercial treaty with the empire. "There must be no question of your loyalty," the priest admonished his pupils. "When Japan calls, you must know that it is Japanese blood that flows in your veins."

The instructor's outbursts against the United States infuriated Daniel, but he kept his feelings to himself. From earliest childhood, he had been taught to treat his elders with respect: According to Japanese tradition, to behave in any other way would bring shame on the entire family. Finally, on one memorable afternoon in 1939, Daniel decided that he could remain silent no longer, even at the risk of disgracing the Inouye name. In the midst of another anti-American

THE ENGLISH STANDARD SYSTEM

During the late 1930s and early 1940s, when Daniel Inouye was a student at McKinley High School, the school was nicknamed "Tokyo High" because its student body was almost entirely Japanese American. In contrast, the student body at the city's other large public high school, Roosevelt, was overwhelmingly haole. Legally, Hawaii's public school system was not supposed to be segregated by race or creed. By the mid-1920s, however, haoles who did not want their children to attend school with nonwhites had found an ingenious way to sidestep the law: the English Standard system.

In response to growing pressure from the archipelago's powerful white minority, in 1924, the Hawaii Department of Public Education started to designate certain schools on the Islands, including Roosevelt High, "English Standard schools." The purported mission of these special schools was to safeguard the purity of spoken English on the archipelago by separating students who spoke "proper," or standard, English from the "corrupting" influence of those who spoke pidgin, a mixture of Japanese, English, and other languages. In order to be admitted to an English Standard school, students had to pass a rigorous oral exam that demonstrated their proficiency in English.

tirade by the old priest, 15-year-old Daniel jumped to his feet and, looking his teacher straight in the eye, shouted, "*I* am an American!" Thoroughly outraged, the priest half-dragged, half-carried Daniel toward the classroom door. "You are a Japanese!" he screamed as he pushed Daniel out and slammed the door behind him. To Daniel's immense relief, when his parents heard about his run-in with the priest, they agreed to let him withdraw from the Japanese school. "I want him to learn the language and traditions of his ancestors," Kame

To no one's surprise, very few Nisei or other children of color on the Islands were able to pass the English Standard exam. During the first half of the twentieth century, virtually all of Hawaii's nonwhite youngsters learned English as their second language—like Daniel Inouye, who spoke only Japanese at home until he was five years old. Also in common with Inouye, whatever English they were able to pick up from their immigrant parents or on the streets of their segregated neighborhoods was almost always in the form of pidgin. By 1940, there were nearly a dozen English Standard schools on the Islands and Hawaii had developed a dual public school system, with white students clustered in the Standard schools and Asian and native Hawaiian children relegated to the other schools. Hawaii's two-tier educational system was not only racially segregated but also inequitable: The better-funded Standard schools had superior facilities and larger staffs. The English Standard system and the racial divisions and inequities that it spawned within Hawaii's public schools lasted for a quarter of a century. Not until 1949, seven years after Daniel Inouye's graduation from "Tokyo High," did the territorial legislature finally begin to phase out the blatantly discriminatory system.

explained to the school's principal, "but we are Americans and shall always remain so."

The year that Daniel dropped out of Japanese school, 1939, was also the year he started to take his American education seriously. Until his sophomore year at McKinley High School, Daniel had set no particular goals for himself beyond graduating and finding a steady job—perhaps as a clerk like his father. The idea of going to college had never even entered his mind. Then, during the fall of 1939, 15-year-old Danny met an extraordinary teacher by the name of Ruth King. Suddenly, he began to envision a very different future for himself than he had ever imagined before.

Although most of the students at McKinley High were of Asian descent, most of the school's faculty were haoles from the mainland. Mrs. King was no exception to the rule. There was one thing that made Mrs. King stand out from Daniel's other teachers, however: She genuinely seemed to believe that he could do more with his life than toil as a field hand or a clerk or at any of the other dead-end jobs to which Japanese Americans were typically relegated. Every afternoon after school, King invited Daniel to work on his grammar with her because his pidgin would hold him back after graduation. Daniel had the ability to excel in college and eventually in a professional career, King insisted, and it was high time that he begin to prepare for his brilliant future.

Inspired by his teacher's faith in him, Daniel decided that he would not only go on to college but to medical school as well. Devoting himself to his studies with a newfound energy, he earned a place in McKinley's most prestigious honor society. To gain some practical medical experience, he also enrolled in an American Red Cross first aid course. He performed so well in it that he was soon invited to teach his own first aid class. As Daniel approached the mid-point of his senior year in December 1941, he was brimming with happy anticipation regarding his postgraduation plans and goals. Little could he have imagined then that his entire world was about to be turned upside down.

In the Wake of Pearl Harbor

Just before 8:00 A.M. on Sunday, December 7, 1941, the Japanese empire launched a devastating surprise attack on the U.S. Pacific Fleet at Pearl Harbor and nearby Oahu airfields. Within two hours, Japan's Imperial bombers had smashed most of the military aircraft on the island, sunk or damaged more than 20 ships, and killed 2,400 U.S. servicemen. Life had never been easy for people of Japanese descent in the United States, and the bombs that rained down on Oahu on December 7 brought them face-to-face with their biggest challenge yet.

Daniel Inouye's first reaction to news of a Japanese air strike was one of disbelief. "It can't be true!" he thought when the reports of Japanese warplanes bombing Oahu blared out from his radio on the morning of December 7. The stories of massive explosions and fires at Pearl Harbor and Hickam Airfield had to be a terrible mistake or a cruel hoax. Daniel knew that relations between the Japanese and the Americans had been worsening rapidly since July, when the U.S. government had cut off all shipments of oil to Japan in response to its recent invasion of French Indochina. Talks between American and Japanese diplomats in Washington, D.C., stalled in October, but Daniel, like most Americans of Japanese descent, hoped that an armed struggle between his country and the country of his ancestors could be avoided.

Daniel's hopes were dashed on that fateful morning, when he and his father rushed out of their house just in time to see three Japanese warplanes flying toward them out of the dense, greasy smoke that enveloped nearby Pearl Harbor. Danny watched the dove-gray planes with the crimson suns on their wings zoom by overhead. His shock and disbelief quickly gave way to grief, shame, and, finally, anger. Daniel felt personally and cruelly betrayed by the land of his ancestors, a nation whose ancient traditions and culture he had always been taught to cherish. "Why had they done it?" he wondered bitterly. "Why couldn't they let us live in peace?"

The insistent ringing of the telephone snapped Daniel out of his angry thoughts. His supervisor at the Red Cross was on the line. He wanted Danny to report immediately to the Lunalilo Elementary School, the first aid station where Danny worked as a part-time instructor. Seconds later, Daniel was on his bicycle pedaling furiously in the direction of Lunalilo, a little more than a mile away in the Asian ghetto of McCully. As he raced through the dingy streets of McCully, Danny felt a momentary rush of elation: Since he had first spotted the Japanese planes, he had wanted nothing more than to show his support for his country and his fellow Americans. He desperately needed to do something—anything—to help. Now, the Red Cross was giving him that chance.

When Daniel finally reached the Lunalilo Elementary School at about 8:30 A.M., he found utter chaos in the first aid station. Everywhere, doctors, nurses, and aid workers were yelling and shoving past each other as they scrambled for stretchers and

Students of the Lunalilo High School in the Waikiki district of Honolulu watch their school burn. The roof of the building was hit accidentally by U.S. antiaircraft shells during the Japanese attack of Pearl Harbor, Hawaii, on December 7, 1941.

medical supplies. As a Red Cross instructor, he had never had to deal with an actual medical emergency, but Daniel boldly plunged into the fray, functioning almost entirely "on adrenaline and instinct," he later recalled.

It soon became obvious to Daniel that all of the wounded at the Lunalilo station were civilians, the vast majority of them Japanese Americans from the surrounding district of McCully. Danny could not have known at the time that his patients' broken bones, lacerations, burns, and other injuries were not the fault of the Japanese bombers, who struck only military targets on December 7. Rather, they were the result of U.S. Navy antiaircraft shells gone astray. Loaded quickly by panicked gun crews who either forgot to use timed fuses or set them incorrectly, the shells had failed to go off in the air. Dozens fell to the ground in Honolulu and nearby areas, landing on homes, businesses, schools, and busy streets. They exploded on impact, often with deadly consequences. Nearly 70 civilians were killed in Oahu during the December 7 attack.

Approximately half an hour after Danny arrived at the Red Cross station, the U.S. fleet at Pearl Harbor was pounded by a second wave of Japanese bombers. Within minutes, a new series of antiaircraft explosions was rocking the crowded McCully district. One shell exploded near the Lunalilo aid station, causing the school's windows to rattle violently. Daniel and two coworkers grabbed a litter—or stretcher—and rushed into the street. Just three blocks from the school, the litter crew encountered its first casualty: A woman, her head almost severed by a piece of shrapnel, lay half-buried in the rubble that had once been her home. A short time later, at the intersection of King and McCully streets, they found a second body, also a woman. To Daniel's horror, she was still clutching the bloody stumps where her legs used to be. All at once, Danny felt numb and mechanical, as though his mind had somehow disconnected from his body. "I moved like an automaton, hardly conscious of what I was doing and totally oblivious of myself. I felt nothing. I did what I had been taught to do and it was only later . . . that I sickened and shuddered as the ghastly images of war flashed again and again in my mind's eye," Inouye recalled of that terrible day more than 25 years later.

Daniel and the other Red Cross workers remained at the Lunalilo station long after the Japanese warplanes had departed Oahu for good late on the morning of December 7. For five days and nights, Danny toiled almost nonstop, tending to the wounded; hunting down meals, clothing, and temporary shelters for the hungry and homeless; and comforting the bereaved. Every now and then, his parents would visit the aid station to check up on him and bring him a change of clothing or a favorite snack. Finally, on December 12, Daniel went home for the first time since the attack.

Danny's responsibilities at the first aid station were far from over, however. President Roosevelt declared war on Japan on December 8 and, a few days later, on Japan's Axis allies, Germany and Italy. After this, staffing Oahu's first aid stations 7 days a week, 24 hours a day, became a top priority for the Red Cross. In the event of another major assault on the island, the stations and their medical personnel would have a critical role to play in caring for civilian casualties. Although Danny was still in high school, his Red Cross supervisor offered him a paid job as a medical aide for the 6:00 P.M. to 6:00 A.M. shift at Lunalilo. As determined as ever to do all he could to assist his nation, Danny quickly accepted. For the remainder of his senior year, he attended classes at McKinley until the early afternoon and then hurried home for a quick nap and meal before heading off to McCully for his 12-hour shift at the first aid center.

Daniel's grueling schedule kept him in a state of exhaustion. His constant weariness was the least of his concerns, however. What really bothered him was the knowledge that many of his fellow Americans did not trust him simply because he resembled the enemy. After the Oahu attack, Hawaii's Issei and Nisei had performed all the same patriotic duties as other islanders, volunteering their time as doctors, nurses, and first aid workers; donating blood to the wounded; buying war bonds; and, if they were in the armed services, reporting promptly to their military units. Nonetheless, after December 7, many Americans automatically considered all ethnic Japanese potential traitors, ready and willing to thwart the United States' wartime efforts. The skeptics assumed that the Nisei and Issei's devotion to their

A wing from a Japanese bomber shot down during the attack on Pearl Harbor fell onto the grounds of the Naval Hospital in Honolulu, Hawaii.

race and ancestral land would win out over their loyalty to the United States. "A Jap is a Jap even after a thousand years and can't become Americanized," one prominent haole business-man remarked after the Pearl Harbor attack.

Immediately after the air raid on Oahu, rumors of sabotage by Japanese Hawaiians began to spread through the Islands like wildfire. It was said that, in the hours before the bombings, local Japanese Americans had been spotted cutting telephone lines, signaling offshore submarines with flares, and even carving ar-rows in sugarcane fields to guide the enemy to critical military targets. Perhaps the most farfetched rumor was that McKinley

High School rings and letter sweaters were found on several of the dead pilots pulled from downed Japanese planes, indicating that the pilots were actually local boys.

At 12:40 P.M. on December 7, 1941, a little less than five hours after the first bombs fell on Pearl Harbor, martial law was declared in Hawaii. It remained in effect almost until the war's end in 1945. With Hawaii under martial law, its new military rulers had the power to do virtually anything they thought necessary to ensure security. It quickly became clear that they were not about to take any chances with the Islands' 158,000 residents of Japanese descent. Japanese-language radio stations and newspapers were strictly censored, and several were shut down altogether. Dozens of Japanese-language schools, Shinto shrines, and Buddhist temples throughout the Islands were also

JAPANESE-AMERICAN INTERNMENT, 1942–1945

Under the terms of Roosevelt's Executive Order 9066, tens of thousands of Nisei and Issei residents of California, western Washington, western Oregon, and southern Arizona were forced to abandon their homes, farms, and businesses in 1942 for "Civilian Assembly Centers," most of which had been hastily constructed on racetracks or fairgrounds. Given a few weeks' notice at most, they were instructed to bring along only the possessions that they could carry. Several weeks later, the internees were moved again to 10 "War Relocation Camps" in isolated areas of Arkansas, Wyoming, Utah, Colorado, Idaho, Arizona, and California. In all, 120,000 men, women, and children of Japanese descent were incarcerated in the closely guarded internment camps between the spring of 1942 and a few months before the war's end in August 1945. Internees faced crowded and primitive living conditions in the camps, where housing typically consisted of crude wooden barracks with tar-paper roofs. Bathrooms and kitchens were communal, and food, which was rationed out at a cost to the government of less than ordered to close their doors. In addition, Japanese Hawaiians were forbidden to own firearms, binoculars, shortwave radio sets, cameras, or any object that could be employed as a signaling device. When local officials learned that Danny's father had purchased a radio with a shortwave band shortly before the Pearl Harbor attack, they ordered him to turn it over and then demolished the costly new set right in front of the family. The fact that Hyotaro had donated blood to the wounded on several occasions or that his son was putting in long hours at the Red Cross aid station made no impression on the government officials. The only thing that mattered to them was the Inouyes' Japanese ancestry.

Throughout World War II, "an extreme degree of fear was present within Hawaii's Japanese community," an observer noted

50 cents per person, was served in mess halls that accommodated up to 300 internees at a time.

In 1944, a landmark legal case was brought before the U.S. Supreme Court to contest the forced evacuation of persons of Japanese descent from the West Coast. In *Korematsu v. United States*, the defendant, California resident and U.S. citizen Fred Korematsu, argued that the government had violated his Fifth Amendment rights on the basis of his ethnic background. In December 1944, the Supreme Court issued its verdict on the case. Six justices voted in favor of the government, arguing that the forced evacuation of persons of Japanese ancestry without due process of law was both "a military necessity" and constitutional. One of the three dissenting judges, Justice Frank Murphy, had this to say about Japanese-American internment, however: "This exclusion of 'all persons of Japanese ancestry, both alien and NON-ALIEN,' from the Pacific Coast area on a plea of military necessity in the absence of martial law ought not to be approved. Such exclusion goes over 'the very brink of constitutional power' and falls into the ugly abyss of racism."

at the time. People feared having their houses searched, being interrogated, and above all, being arrested and imprisoned on suspicion of disloyalty. They had reason to be afraid: Nearly 1,500 Japanese Hawaiians—most of them Buddhist priests, Japanese-language school instructors, international businessmen, and others who were perceived to have especially strong ties to their birth country—were hauled in for questioning during the weeks and months after the attack on Pearl Harbor. Although there was no evidence that any of those suspected had carried out a single act of sabotage or espionage, by the war's end, less than half of them had been released. After the arrests of many of their community's most prominent members, rumors began to circulate among Japanese Hawaiians that merely possessing Japanese books, records, and other objects was considered suspicious and could result in imprisonment. In order to prove their "Americanness," many people destroyed or buried anything that might make them appear to be overly attached to their Japanese heritage, including treasured family heirlooms such as samurai swords, kimonos, and even photographs of relatives in the old country.

The war years were difficult for people of Japanese ancestry who lived in Hawaii, but, as residents of Hawaii, they were far better off than their Issei and Nisei counterparts on the mainland. On February 19, 1942, President Roosevelt issued Executive Order 9066, which authorized U.S. military commanders to designate areas of the country as military sectors from which anyone considered a threat to national security could be excluded without due process of law. Roosevelt's order set the stage for one of the most notorious episodes in U.S. history: the forced removal of 120,000 men, women, and children of Japanese ancestry, most of them American born, from their West Coast homes to specially constructed internment camps in remote interior regions of the country.

During the early months of the war, powerful officials in the government urged the confinement of all individuals of Japanese background who resided in Hawaii on the West Coast. At the very least, argued Secretary of the Navy Frank Knox, persons of Japanese ancestry who lived on Oahu, with its vital military bases, should be evacuated for the duration of the war. Hawaii's military governor, General Delos Emmons, strongly opposed any scheme to resettle large numbers of ethnic Japanese islanders, however. Emmons even went so far as to publicly assure the archipelago's Issei and Nisei residents that, under his watch, there would be no mass internment of Hawaiian residents solely on the basis of ethnic background: "No person, be he citizen or alien, need worry, provided he is not connected with subversive elements. . . . While we have been subjected to a serious attack by a ruthless and treacherous enemy, we must remember that this is America and we must do things the American Way. We must distinguish between loyalty and disloyalty among our people."

In truth, the relocation of Hawaii's Issei and Nisei population was highly impractical, as Emmons well knew. As he repeatedly pointed out to the Roosevelt Administration, the mass internment of Japanese American islanders was bound to spell economic disaster for Hawaii. At the time of the Pearl Harbor attack, persons of Japanese descent represented 37 percent of the Islands' total population and the majority of Hawaii's agricultural laborers, transportation workers, and skilled tradesmen. Hawaii simply could not afford to lose such a vital part of its labor force, Emmons asserted, particularly during wartime.

6

"4-C"

Fortunately for the nearly 160,000 Nisei and Issei who called Hawaii home at the beginning of World War II, Emmons persuaded the federal government that a large-scale evacuation of ethnic Japanese islanders would not be in Hawaii's—or the nation's—best interest. Consequently, in September 1942, Inouye was able to enroll at the University of Hawaii in Honolulu as a premedical student, as he had planned. He was now one step closer to fulfilling his dream of becoming a surgeon. Still, Inouye felt depressed and deeply frustrated. Now that he had graduated from high school and turned 18, he wanted nothing more than to join the armed forces and fight for his country. As an American of Japanese descent, however, he did not possess that right.

In March 1942, the War Department had officially declared all Japanese Americans "4-C," or "enemy aliens," meaning that they could neither volunteer nor be drafted for military service. "That really hit me," Inouye recalled more than six decades later. "I considered myself patriotic, and to

When the U.S. government finally allowed Japanese Americans to participate in its armed forces, Hawaiian residents responded in droves. In this photograph, men crowd into Selective Service Board No. 9 in Waipahu, Hawaii, to enlist in the U.S. Army's combat regiment of Japanese Americans.

be told you could not put on a uniform, that was an insult." Soon, he had joined thousands of his fellow Nisei in a petition and letter-writing campaign to convince the government to let them defend their nation as so many other young Americans already were.

Finally, in early 1943, the Nisei's determined campaign to rid themselves of their 4-C status paid off. President Roosevelt called for 1,000 volunteers from Hawaii and 3,000 from the mainland to form a new, all-Japanese-American unit, the 442nd Regimental Combat Team. In Hawaii, the response to

Roosevelt's announcement was overwhelming: Nearly 10,000 Nisei volunteered, "representing about 85 percent of the eligible young men of Japanese ancestry on the islands," Daniel Inouye later noted in Thomas Wilborn's book *World War II*. On the mainland, where the majority of the Japanese population was being held in crude and heavily guarded internment camps, however, barely more than 1,000 Nisei volunteered for the new unit. Forced to revise its numbers, the army ultimately inducted 800 mainland and 2,686 Hawaiian Nisei for the new unit. Daniel was originally turned down by recruiters because his work at the Red Cross aid station was deemed critical to the war effort, but, in March 1943, he became number 2,685 of the Hawaiian inductees.

Two days after learning that he had been selected for the new all-Nisei unit, Daniel said goodbye to his father at Schofield Barracks, where the inductees had been ordered to gather prior to their departure from Hawaii. Danny never forgot Hyotaro Inouye's parting words to him that spring morning. "Do you know what *on* means in Japanese?" Hyotaro asked. Daniel replied that he did: *On* is a concept that lies at the very core of Japanese culture and ethics. It says that, when a man or woman receives an important favor or gift, he or she is forever indebted to the giver of that gift. "The Inouyes have great *on* for America," Hyotaro continued. "It has been good to us." Now, Hyotaro told his eldest son, even though he would never have chosen it this way, it was Daniel "who must return the goodness of this country at any cost. This is a matter of honor."

In mid-April, after a short stopover in San Francisco, Daniel and the other Hawaiian members of the 442nd arrived at Camp Shelby, Mississippi, to begin what would be a 10-month training period. Although some of the white soldiers at the base taunted Daniel and his comrades, calling them "Japs," the Nisei troops were pleasantly surprised by the warm welcome they

Daniel Inouye is shown in this undated photo in his U.S. Army uniform. A member of the highly decorated all-Nisei 442nd Regimental Combat Team, Inouye served from 1943 to 1947.

received from the white communities near Camp Shelby. The men of the 442nd had been deeply apprehensive about being stationed in the South; they knew that discrimination against blacks was still common and severe. "We'd only heard about

Between the Generations

INTO THE MELTING POT

In the foreword to *Encyclopedia of Japanese American History* Daniel Inouye poignantly described the experiences of the Issei and their U.S.-born children, the Nisei:

Japanese Americans have played an active part in the development of this country for over 100 years. This history begins during the latter part of the 19th century when the Issei immigrants came in increasing numbers. . . . The Issei worked hard in the fields, factories, forests, cities and on the seas and made vital contributions to the plantation economy in Hawaii and to the industrial development of western America.

The immigrant Isseis' quick adjustment to the work opportunities and adaptation to life in America were made in spite of hardships. Through a series of laws they were deprived of the most elementary civil rights: citizenship, owning or leasing land and interracial marriage. . . . The Issei promoted a code of ethics involving reciprocal obligations, mutual responsibility, respect for elders and the value of hard work. They taught these values and attitudes to their children, the Nisei. . . .

Perhaps the single most critical event in [Issei and Nisei] history was the incarceration of the Japanese Americans during World War II. . . . Although not a single case of espionage or sabotage was ever attributed to Japanese Americans, they were singled out, uprooted from their homes and exiled to desolate internment centers. . . . It is indeed amazing that under these circumstances Nisei men and women volunteered for service in the armed forces to prove their loyalty to the United States of America. . . .

the lynchings," Inouye revealed years later, "but to our surprise these people were very good to us. We were invited to weekend parties and picnics, and for the first time in my life I danced with a white girl."

After the end of World War II, the Nisei gradually came to enjoy greater economic, social, and educational opportunities and were able to make important gains in fields that had once been all but closed to them such as law, medicine, and government. This was at least in part because of the widely publicized battlefield exploits of Japanese American soldiers such as Daniel Inouye. The Nisei's children, the Sansei (third generation), and their grandchildren, the Yonsei (fourth generation), are among the most thoroughly assimilated of all Asian-American groups. They attend school, work, and reside in urban and, to a lesser extent, rural communities across the United States alongside Americans from a variety of racial, ethnic, and cultural groups. The Sansei and Yonsei are also marrying people outside of their ethnic group in record numbers. As a result, in recent decades, more children have been born in the United States to couples in which only one parent is ethnic Japanese than to couples in which both are.

From the enactment of the Johnson-Reed Act in 1924 until the passage of the groundbreaking Immigration Act of 1965, Japanese immigration to the United States remained at a trickle. Even after the old restrictions against Japanese immigration were lifted in the mid-1960s, relatively few Japanese chose to settle permanently in the United States. Today, no more than 10,000 new Japanese immigrants arrive in the nation each year. In comparison to the Issei of the late nineteenth and early twentieth centuries, the new immigrants are better educated and more prosperous. The majority come to the United States not in search of employment opportunities but rather to join a spouse who is a U.S. citizen.

Relations between the soldiers of the 442nd and Camp Shelby's white neighbors may have been cordial, but relations between the two groups of Nisei who made up the regiment were a different matter. From their very first day in boot camp, there was tension between the 442nd's mainland members and its Hawaiian members. The mainlanders dubbed the islanders "buddaheads," from the pidgin term *buta-head*, which means "pig headed." They also scoffed at the Nisei's broken English. The islanders accused the mainlanders of being stuck up and derisively nicknamed them "katonks," after the hollow sound that their heads supposedly made when they hit the floor during a fistfight. Soon, the bad feeling between the two Nisei groups had escalated to the point that army officials seriously contemplated disbanding the 442nd.

Finally, someone in the military high command had an idea about how to bring the regiment together. A group of buddaheads would be sent to Arkansas, the site of the nearest Japanese internment compound, for a weekend excursion. The proud katonks had never revealed the dismal conditions in which their families and other mainland Japanese Americans were being forced to live to their Hawaiian counterparts. Indeed, Daniel and the other Hawaiian members of the 442nd who were invited to go on the Arkansas excursion assumed that they were visiting because the town had an unusually large Japanese-American community. They were looking forward to a weekend of good food, dances, and pretty girls. When the soldiers arrived at the Rohwer Relocation Center, their pleasant fantasy was abruptly shattered. More than a half a century later, Daniel Inouye could vividly recall his first introduction to a Japanese-American internment camp: "In the distance, we could see rows of barracks surrounded by high barbed-wire fences with machine-gun towers. . . . When we finally came to the gate, we were ordered to get off the trucks. We were in uniform and were confronted by men in similar uniforms but they had rifles with bayonets."

Students pose for a photographer at the Rohwer Relocation Center in rural Arkansas. The Rohwer Center was the internment center that Daniel Inouye and his Nisei comrades from the 442nd visited in 1943 to learn of the treatment of Japanese Americans on the U.S. mainland.

Inouye and his comrades soon discovered that the heavily guarded Japanese-American families of Rohwer had rationed their food in order to have something to share with their visitors. They even offered to let the soldiers stay in their cramped barracks for the night while they slept on the cafeteria floor, but the embarrassed men declined, saying that they would bunk down in their trucks instead. That evening, the camp residents threw a party for the Hawaiians, "but everything was very somber," Inouye recalled. "How can you dance under those circumstances?" When Inouye and his buddies rolled out of Rohwer the next morning, the laughter and singing that had filled their trucks on the way to Arkansas was replaced by silent reflection. Every man, Inouye believes, was thinking the same thing: If they and their families had been torn from their homes and locked up in one of those dreary camps, would they still have volunteered to fight?

After the trip to Rohwer, Daniel and his Hawaiian comrades never again saw the katonks in the same light. "Suddenly," he wrote, "our respect, admiration, and love for our . . . brothers rose to phenomenal heights." Almost overnight, the soldiers of the 442nd became united. "The regiment was formed," Inouye recalled, "and we were ready to fight anybody."

7

"Go for Broke"

World War II would be a time of unprecedented hardship and despair for the more than quarter-million Issei and Nisei who resided on American soil during the conflict. For the band of young Japanese American warriors to which Daniel Inouye belonged from 1943 on, the long and bloody contest between the United States and their ancestral land would also be their time of greatest glory. The heroic deeds of Inouye's all-Nisei 442nd Regimental Combat Team received widespread acclaim and were to play a critical role in helping the Japanese-American community achieve new political and economic gains during the postwar era, particularly in the part of the United States with the largest ethnic Japanese population: Hawaii.

In May 1944, after nearly a year of training, the men of the 442nd finally headed off to Italy and to war. Early the next month, they arrived just north of Rome at the town of Civitavecchia, where they absorbed the army's other all-Nisei unit, the 100th Battalion. Composed of former Hawaii National Guardsmen, the 100th had fought valiantly in Italy over the past several months. It had suffered so many casualties in the process that it had earned the nickname "Purple Heart Battalion" and the admiration of the army high command. (The Purple Heart Medal is awarded to any member of the U.S. armed forces who is wounded or killed in an armed conflict.)

Inspired by the 100th's battlefield exploits, Inouye and the other newly arrived members of the 442nd were determined to earn a reputation for extraordinary courage under fire as well. "We had to demonstrate to our fellow Americans and to the government that they had made a mistake when they considered us to be disloyal and not good citizens," Inouye said after the war. "And we fully realized at the very outset that to demonstrate this would mean the shedding of blood, but we were prepared for that." For their regimental motto, the soldiers of the 442nd took the Hawaiian gambler's traditional cry: "Go for Broke!" In other words, they were ready and willing to do whatever it took to win, no matter the cost. As it turned out, the cost was heavy.

During three months of fierce fighting in the Italian countryside, Inouye was promoted from lead scout to corporal and finally to sergeant. At this time, the 442nd was sent to eastern France. There, the men seized the towns of Bruyères, Belmont, and Biffontaine from the Nazis in vicious house-to-house combat. After just two days of rest, in late October, the 442nd was ordered to march to France's Vosges Mountains to perform what would become their most celebrated mission: the rescue of 211 members of the 1st Battalion of the 141st Infantry Regiment of the Texas National Guard, better known as the "Lost Battalion."

By the time that the 442nd was called in to help, the Lost Battalion had been trapped in the Vosges for nearly a week, surrounded by several units of heavily armed German troops. Two battalions from the Lone Star State had already been sent to retrieve their fellow Texans, but both had been thrown back.

Japanese American infantrymen of the 442nd regiment run for cover from German artillery fire during a battle with Nazi forces in April 1945, shortly before the end of the war in Europe.

For three long days, the Nisei soldiers pushed through rugged mountain and forest terrain as enemy shells burst all around them. Finally, on the fourth day, they broke through the German lines. During the assault, the 442nd suffered 800 casualties, including 300 dead—a high price to pay to save 211 men. The unit had performed with extraordinary courage and tenacity, however, and Daniel Inouye, for one, had no regrets: "We knew that from that moment on, no one could ever, ever, question our loyalty and our love for our country," he explained to an interviewer years later.

Inouye's performance during the fighting in France was so exemplary that the army awarded him a field commission as a second lieutenant, making him the youngest lieutenant in his entire regiment. Lieutenant Inouye and the 442nd spent several relatively uneventful months near the city of Nice guarding a section of the French-Italian border. Then, in the spring of 1945, they were sent to northern Italy to take part in the final Allied assault on German strongholds in the Apennine Mountains. The Apennines campaign would prove to be a major turning point in Daniel Inouye's military career and in his life.

Early on the morning of April 21, 1945, Inouye led his platoon in a daring raid on a heavily fortified ridge near San Terenzo, Italy, named Colle Musatello. In the face of heavy enemy fire, the young lieutenant guided his men up the dangerous slope, destroying two German machine gun nests along the way. When Inouye was within 40 yards of the main German position, he suddenly felt a massive punch to his right side. He later discovered that he had been shot in the abdomen and that the bullet had barely missed his spine before exiting through his back.

Although gravely wounded, Inouye pushed on ahead of his men toward the enemy stronghold. Just as he was preparing to lob a grenade into the bunker, a blast from a German rifle grenade tore into his right arm, all but blowing it off. Even this did not stop him. In a flash, he had pried the grenade out of his frozen right fingers and hurled it at the sniper. Firing left-handed with his submachine gun, Inouye continued to close in on the bunker until a bullet struck his right shin and sent him tumbling back down the hill. Although in excruciating pain and bleeding heavily, he refused medical evacuation, insisting that he would not leave the battle scene until German resistance was broken and he knew that his men were safe. Owing in large measure to the young Nisei officer's extraordinary courage and leadership, by the end of the day, both the ridge and the key road junction that the German gunners had been guarding had fallen under American control, all without the loss of a single soldier from Inouye's platoon.

Inouye spent several months after the battle at Colle Musatello in and out of surgery at various army field hospitals in Italy. As he had feared from the start, his right arm could not be saved. The war in Europe ended on May 8, 1945, not even three weeks after he was wounded, but for his heroism that April day, the lieutenant was awarded the Distinguished Service Cross and three Purple Hearts. Many in his regiment were convinced that, if he had not been Japanese American, Inouye would have been awarded the military's highest honor, the Congressional Medal of Honor. Just one Nisei soldier, 22-year-old Private First Class Sadao Munemori of California, received the Medal of Honor during World War II. Munemori was awarded the medal posthumously (after his death) for throwing himself onto a German grenade to save the lives of two of his American comrades on April 5, 1945, near Seravezza, Italy.

Shortly before the Japanese surrender and the end of the war in the Pacific on August 14, 1945, Inouye was shipped back to the United States to begin to learn how to live one-armed. For the next 11 months, his home was a hotel in Atlantic City, New Jersey, that had been converted into a rehabilitation center for wounded soldiers. During those months, he became adept at using his left hand for everyday tasks such as shaving, dressing, using a knife and fork, writing, and opening letters. In mid-1946, Daniel was transferred to Percy Jones Army Hospital in Battle Creek, Michigan, for nine more months of rehabilitation. There, Daniel's "can-do" attitude and outstanding card-playing skills won the admiration of another patient who had also been severely wounded in Italy just weeks before the end of the war in Europe. His name was Bob Dole, and eventually he would serve with Inouye in the U.S. Senate. Bridge was a favorite pastime of the Percy Jones patients, and, in his memoirs, Dole described

"I NEVER GOT USED TO IT"

One day during the summer of 1944, Daniel Inouye was leading a patrol in the Italian countryside. As the patrol approached what appeared to be a deserted farmhouse, three German snipers suddenly opened fire on them from an upstairs window, killing the lead scout. The patrol retaliated by firing a bazooka right through the window. Rushing upstairs, Inouye and his men immediately spotted two of the Germans, their bodies literally torn to pieces by the bazooka. The third, Inouye recalled in his autobiography, "had been thrown back across the room, and he lay sprawled against the wall, nearly senseless, with one leg shredded and twisted completely around. 'Kamerad,' [Comrade], he whispered, smiling sadly. 'Kamerad.'" Then the wounded man slowly reached into his jacket.

Thinking that the German was going for a pistol, Inouye reacted instinctively, pumping three rifle shots directly into his chest. Years later, Daniel's memories of what happened next were still painfully vivid: "He jerked each time, and the last time, as he toppled over, his hand sprang spasmodically out from his tunic, and he held up a snapshot, clutching it in death. There was a woman in it, a pretty woman, and two little kids, and there was a handwritten inscription: 'Deine Dichliebende Frau, Heidi' [Your loving wife, Heidi]."

Inouye never forgot that day in Italy when he "made a widow and two orphans"; nor would he ever truly reconcile himself to killing other men in combat, as deeply as he believed in the Allied cause: "I never got used to it," he wrote more than two decades after the war's end:

Deep down, I think no one did. We pretended to be callused and insensitive because we understood the fatal consequences of caring too much. You were no good to your men; you were through as a soldier if you cared too much. But hidden in the core of every man's being, there must have been a wound, a laceration of the spirit, and the abrasives of war rubbed against it every day and you thought that even if you lived, and the years passed, it would never stop bleeding.

the upbeat Inouye as "the best bridge player I'd ever seen. I marveled as I watched him whip everyone in the ward, playing with only one hand, his cards placed in a rack in front of him."

Dole and Inouye became close friends during their months at Percy Jones. Years later, Inouye gave Dole credit for steering him toward a career in public service. With his longtime dream of becoming a surgeon dashed, Inouye was not sure what to do with the rest of his life. Coincidentally, Dole's right arm was mangled on an Italian battlefield just a few miles from the spot where Inouye was wounded. Before his injury, the Kansas native had also hoped to be a surgeon. When Inouye asked his friend if he had come up with a new plan for the future, Dole said that he was contemplating attending law school and working as an attorney for a few years before running for the state legislature, and eventually, the U.S. Congress. Inspired by what he later called "the Dole Plan," for the first time Inouye began to seriously consider entering politics.

Another close friend from his rehabilitation days, Japanese-Hawaiian veteran Sakae Takahashi, also encouraged Inouye's interest in public service. After spending two years overseas fighting to make the world safe for democracy, Takahashi was impatient with the second-class status that his people were still forced to endure back home. The quickest way for Japanese Hawaiians to achieve full economic, educational, and social equality, he argued, was for the Nisei to take a more active role in territorial politics—as both voters and lawmakers. Takahashi's words made a profound impression on Daniel Inouye. "What Sakae was saying and what I came to believe with all my heart and soul was that the time had come for us to step forward," Inouye wrote. "We had fought for that right with all the furious patriotism in our bodies and now we didn't want to go back to the plantation. . . .We wanted to take our full place in society, to make the greatest contribution of which we were capable."

In May 1947, after 20 months of rehabilitation, Inouye was honorably discharged from the army with the rank of captain. The previous summer, the Nisei veterans of the 442nd Regimental Combat Team had gathered at the White House for a special review by President Harry Truman in recognition of their battlefield achievements. Often cited as the most decorated military unit for its size and length of service in U.S. history, the 442nd were granted 7 Presidential Unit Citations and more than 18,000 individual awards, including nearly 9,500 Purple Hearts. By the time of the White House ceremony in July 1946, stirring accounts of the 442nd's remarkable heroism had appeared in dozens of American newspapers and magazines and the unit had earned the admiration of tens of thousands of ordinary citizens, Asian and non-Asian alike. "You fought for the free nations of the world. . . . You fought not only the enemy, you fought prejudice, and you have won," Truman told the men before presenting them with their seventh and last Presidential Unit Citation.

As Inouye quickly discovered, however, not all of his fellow countrymen were sufficiently impressed by the courage of the Nisei soldiers to cast off their prejudices and resentments toward people of Japanese descent. On his way home to Hawaii in May 1947, Inouye tried to get a haircut in a California barbershop. Although he was wearing his army uniform—covered with medals, ribbons, and his new captain's bars—and there was a hook where his right hand should have been, the Caucasian barber refused to wait on him. "We don't cut Jap hair," the man snarled. "I was tempted to slash him with my hook," Inouye later confided to an interviewer, "but then I thought about all the work the 442nd had done and I just said, 'I feel sorry for you,' and walked out. I went home without a haircut."

Countless Japanese Americans on the mainland felt the sting of racism for years after World War II, but, in postwar Hawaii, Truman's claim that the Nisei veterans had fought prejudice and

President Harry S Truman reviewed the Japanese-American 442nd
Regimental Combat Team during a special ceremony held on the White
House lawn on July 15, 1946.

won seemed a great deal closer to the truth. Because of their
wartime sacrifices, Japanese Hawaiians enjoyed new respect
from their fellow Islanders after 1945. Between them, the all–
Japanese-American 442nd and 100th units furnished fully 60
percent of Hawaii's fighting forces, 80 percent of the Islands'
war dead, and 88 percent of its wounded. The 442nd's turnover
rate due to battlefield casualties was so high that, eventually, it
required 12,000 Nisei—the majority of them from Hawaii—to
fill the unit's original 4,000 places. Supported by the admiration

and gratitude of their fellow Islanders, the returning war heroes were able to serve as an important force for change in Hawaii after World War II. Largely because of the inspiration and leadership provided by Daniel Inouye and other Nisei veterans, the decade after the end of the war would encompass unheard-of educational, economic, and political gains for Hawaii's large Japanese-American community.

In the autumn of 1947, Daniel Inouye enrolled at the University of Hawaii as a prelaw student, majoring in government and economics. Like tens of thousands of other young men of his era, he relied on the generous financial benefits provided to World War II veterans by the G.I. Bill to fund his college education.

When he was not in class or studying, Inouye could usually be found volunteering at the headquarters of the Honolulu County Democratic Committee. He had been talked into joining the Democratic Party by the chairman of the Honolulu County Committee, John Burns, a former police captain with strong ties to Hawaii's Japanese community. Burns had won the undying gratitude of the archipelago's Issei and Nisei when he became one of the few haole officials to publicly express his confidence in their loyalty during the tense days after the Pearl Harbor attack.

Since Hawaii's annexation by the United States in 1898, its political life had been dominated by the Republican Party—the party of the Islands' sugar planters and other haole elite. Nonetheless, Burns persuaded Inouye that, with the support of Hawaii's substantial Japanese population, the Democratic Party could not only rise again but could also become the vehicle by which Japanese Hawaiians finally achieved meaningful social and economic reforms and the equality of opportunity that had always been denied to them.

Around the same time, Daniel Inouye met a young Nisei by the name of Margaret Awamura. Unusually well educated for a woman of her era, Awamura held a master's degree from Columbia University and worked as a speech instructor at the

University of Hawaii. Inouye was so smitten by the intelligent and charming teacher that he asked her to marry him on their second date. She accepted, and, on June 12, 1948, Daniel Inouye and Margaret Awamura were married at the Harris Memorial Methodist Church in Honolulu. Although she did not share her new spouse's passion for politics, Margaret Awamura Inouye never complained about the long hours Daniel put in at the Democratic headquarters trying to drum up support for his struggling party. From the very beginning, she understood that politics was and would always be an integral part of her husband's life.

After Daniel's graduation from the University of Hawaii in 1950, the Inouyes immediately left Oahu for Washington, D.C., where Daniel planned to attend George Washington University Law School. As he later explained, his interest in studying the law was directly linked to his political aspirations: "From the first, I thought about the law in its purest sense, the law of the land. I wanted to become a lawyer so I could go into politics."

Shortly after arriving in Washington, Inouye visited the headquarters of the Democratic National Committee (DNC), the U.S. Democratic Party's principal campaign and fund-raising organization, to volunteer his services. "I told them that I wanted no pay," Daniel recalled, "only the experience of working close to the grass roots, of learning enough so that when I went back to Hawaii I could bring something more than just my amateur standing and a brand new law degree." Inouye's supervisors at the DNC were so impressed by the young law student's dedication and enthusiasm that they were soon allowing him to sit in on high-level fund-raising, publicity planning, and strategy meetings.

In the fall of 1952, with Daniel having earned his JD (doctor of jurisprudence) degree in just two years, the Inouyes returned to Oahu. Daniel was anxious to get back to work rebuilding Hawaii's Democratic Party. For nearly a year, he divided his time between cramming for the Hawaii bar exam and volunteering for the Territorial Democratic Central Committee, now chaired by his old friend John Burns. Soon after passing the bar exam in August 1953, Inouye was appointed assistant public prosecutor for the city and county of Honolulu by Honolulu Mayor John Wilson, one of the few Democrats who held a major political office on Oahu during the early 1950s. Inouye was grateful for the appointment, but it turned out that he would not remain a public prosecutor for long.

The year 1953, when Inouye began to work for the public prosecutor's office, was an exciting and hopeful time for Democrats in Hawaii. Although Republicans remained in control of both the territorial House and Senate, Democrats had captured several new legislative seats in the November 1952 elections and had every reason to anticipate an even stronger showing in the 1954 races. Over the past several years, the party had enjoyed increasing success in attracting groups that had long felt used and excluded by the Republican elite, including Japanese and other Asian Americans, native Hawaiians, and plantation and dock workers of many ethnic and racial backgrounds. The growing appeal of the Democratic Party among Islanders of Asian descent was particularly significant: Hawaii had undergone a major demographic (population) shift over the past decade as a whole generation of U.S.-born Filipino, Korean, Chinese, and Japanese Americans came of age. Adding to this large new pool of prospective Democratic voters were the Issei, who had finally been granted the right to U.S. citizenship in late 1952, when Congress approved legislation that made immigrants of all races eligible for naturalization.

During the summer of 1954, the Territorial Democratic Central Committee began to compile a roster of candidates for the upcoming elections. It featured many new faces to the Hawaiian political scene. Nisei candidates—particularly Nisei veterans—figured prominently on the list and included Sakae Takahashi and Spark M. Matsunaga, both highly decorated

The loss of his arm in combat led to Inouye's discharge from the U.S. Army. His dreams of becoming a surgeon dashed, he decided to devote his life to politics and public service.

members of the 442nd Regimental Combat Team; Russell Kono, who fought in the China-Burma-India Theater; and Daniel Inouye. Although at first reluctant to run for a major office so early in his political career, Inouye agreed to campaign for a seat in the territorial House from his home district, the Fourth, at Burns's urging.

The contest for the Fourth District quickly turned ugly when, during a public debate, Inouye's Republican opponent accused him of being soft on Communism. In 1954, the United States was in the grip of a "red scare." During the red scare, fears of an external attack on the United States by the Communist-led Soviet Union were intertwined with fears of activity from within by alleged "reds," or Communists, in organized labor, the federal government, and the entertainment business. In the intensely anti-Communist climate of the early 1950s, "red baiting" (accusing someone of being a Communist sympathizer) often proved to be an effective tactic to harm the reputation of political rivals. For Inouye's haole opponent, the strategy turned out to be a dismal failure. The highly decorated veteran of the "Go for Broke" regiment was not about to take what he viewed as a direct assault on his patriotism lying down. "I cannot help wondering," Inouye declared, "whether the people of Hawaii will not think it strange that the only weapon in the Republican arsenal is to label as communists men so recently returned from defending liberty on the firing lines in Italy and France." Then, dramatically holding up his empty right sleeve, Inouye continued amidst thunderous applause from the audience: "I gave this arm to fight fascists. If my country wants the other one to fight communists, it can have it!" When the votes for the Fourth District were tallied a few weeks later, Inouye had won by a substantial margin, as had four of the other five Democratic candidates for the legislature from his home district.

The Democratic Party captured more than just the five seats in the Fourth District that fall: When the ballots were in, Democratic candidates had won 22 of the 30 seats in the territorial House and 10 of the 15 Senate seats in what came to be known as "the Democratic revolution of 1954." Clearly, the days of one-party rule were over in Hawaii. It was also evident after the elections that Japanese Americans had become a force to be reckoned with in Island politics. In 1946, only six Nisei were elected to the territorial legislature. Just eight years later, Nisei held one out of every two seats in the House and the Senate alike. "We wanted to take our full place in society, to make the greatest contribution of which we were capable," Daniel Inouye had said of his fellow Japanese Hawaiians at the end of World War II. In November 1954, it appeared that that dream was being realized at long last.

8

Becoming a National Figure

D aniel Inouye served as majority leader in Hawaii's territorial House of Representatives from 1955 until 1958. He then moved on to the territorial Senate in 1959. Now that the Democrats controlled the territorial legislature, they devoted themselves to a wide-ranging economic and social reform program, including the creation of Hawaii's first graduated income tax, expansion of the territory's slum clearance program, and increased government funding for public schools. As important as these reform measures were to the party, there was nothing that the Democrats—and many Republican as well—desired more for their homeland than statehood.

The first statehood bill for the Territory of Hawaii was introduced to Congress just 20 years after the Islands became a U.S. possession in 1898. Over the next three decades, dozens of similar bills followed. Nonetheless, in 1954, when Daniel Inouye was first elected to the territorial House of Representatives, Hawaii still was not a state. By the 1950s, most

Islanders were deeply frustrated by the archipelago's seemingly permanent status as a U.S. territory. As long as Hawaii was denied full admission to the Union, they complained, its inhabitants would remain second-class citizens, without any real voice in Washington, D.C. As residents of a territory, Islanders were barred from taking part in presidential elections and their sole delegate in Congress, although allowed to introduce bills, had no vote. Hawaiians did not even have the privilege of electing their own governor; the person who filled this position was chosen by the president and confirmed by the Senate.

Although Hawaii's distance from the mainland was often cited as the chief reason for withholding statehood, many Congressmen were clearly more concerned about the racially diverse population than about the location. Because Hawaii had a nonwhite majority, they feared that its people could not be readily assimilated into the predominantly Caucasian United States. Even after Islanders—particularly Japanese Hawaiians—more than proved their loyalty to the United States during World War II, some in Congress continued to argue that Hawaii was too "Oriental" in culture and racial makeup to be granted statehood.

After he was elected as the Islands' congressional delegate in 1956, Inouye's old friend John Burns played a key role in finally overcoming racist opposition to Hawaiian statehood in Congress. When a Southern congressman asked Burns how he could expect the federal government to admit Hawaii to the Union when barely one-third of its residents were white, Burns reportedly replied, "I've studied the Constitution of the United States and nowhere does it say that the United States is for Caucasians. . . . My constituents may not look like yours, but let me assure you that they are as good Americans, if not better Americans than your constituents." In March 1959, Burns's determined lobbying, along with the Islands' booming postwar economy, convinced Congress to finally accept Hawaii as

President Dwight Eisenhower helps unfurl the new 50-star U.S. flag in Washington, D.C., on August 21, 1959, after he signed a proclamation making Hawaii the 50th state of the union. Daniel Inouye stands at far right. Eisenhower's proclamation capped a century-long effort by what was once an island kingdom.

a state. Three months later, Islanders voted to ratify Congress's action by a ratio of 17 to 1, and, on August 21, 1959, President Dwight Eisenhower officially signed the Hawaii Admission Act into law.

During the summer of 1959, special elections were held on the Islands to fill the new political offices that came with statehood. Inouye ran for Hawaii's single seat in the House of Representatives and won by a huge majority over his Republican opponent. Hiram Fong, a Republican businessman of Chinese descent, was elected to the Senate, along with Democrat Oren E. Long, a former territorial governor. Inouye became the first Japanese American to serve in the House of Representatives, and Fong was not only the first Chinese American but also the first Asian American to be elected to the Senate. (Inouye was not the first Asian American to win a seat in the House of Representatives. That distinction went to India-born Dalip Singh Saund, who was elected to the House from California's 29th District in 1956.)

Keenly aware of the historic significance of the election, shortly after his victory, Inouye felt moved to visit the National Memorial Cemetery of the Pacific, also called the "Punchbowl," in Honolulu, where many of his fallen comrades from the 442nd had been laid to rest. "I wanted to assure them that I would never let them down, never dishonor the cause and the country for which they had given so much," Inouye recalled many years later. "I wanted to promise them that I was not going to Washington to represent the 442nd, or the Nisei, or any other separate group. I was going to represent all the people of Hawaii, and I asked God's help in this, the greatest undertaking of my life."

Two days after President Eisenhower signed the Hawaii Admission Act, Daniel Inouye was sworn in as the Islands' first congressman by Speaker of the House Sam Rayburn. Congressman Leo O'Brien of New York later commemorated that historic and poignant moment in the Congressional Record:

> The House was very still, it was about to witness the swearing in, not only of the first Congressman from Hawaii, but the first American of Japanese descent to serve in either House of Congress.

"Raise your right hand and repeat after me," intoned Speaker Rayburn.

The hush deepened as the young Congressman raised not his right hand but his left, and he repeated the oath of office.

There was no right hand, Mr. Speaker. It had been lost in combat by that young American soldier in World War II. Who can deny that, at that moment, a ton of prejudice slipped quietly to the floor of the House of Representatives.

Fortunately for Inouye, Speaker Rayburn became his loyal mentor in the House, even securing the freshman congressman a spot on the powerful Banking and Currency Committee. Barely a year after arriving in Washington, the popular young war veteran was reelected to Congress with the largest number of votes ever won by a candidate in Hawaii. Soon after the landslide election, Rayburn offered Inouye a place on the prestigious House Foreign Affairs Committee, an assignment guaranteed to bring him national attention. Inouye was more concerned with doing what he thought was best for Hawaii than he was with furthering his own political career, however. During the early 1960s, Hawaii's economy was dominated by agriculture, and Inouye reasoned that he could contribute the most to his state by taking a seat on the less glamorous Agriculture Committee instead. There, he could help secure policies favorable to the Islands' vital sugar, pineapple, and cattle industries.

In 1962, after spending a little more than three years in the House, Daniel Inouye became the first Japanese-American senator in U.S. history when he easily defeated his Republican opponent, Benjamin F. Dillingham III. "I was going to the Senate, to the very highest reaches of my government, I, Dan Inouye, who had been raised in respectable poverty and whose father had been born in a tiny Japanese village," the new senator from Hawaii wrote:

Daniel and Margaret Inouye wave upon arrival at Friendship Airport in Washington, D.C., on August 9, 1959. Soon after, Inouye became the first Japanese American to serve in the U.S. Congress.

My face and eyes and shape would be different from those of my colleagues. . . . But the fact is that there was really not so great a difference between my story and the stories of millions of other Americans who had come to this land from Ireland and Italy and Poland and Greece. They had come because America would permit any man to aspire to the topmost limits of his own talent and energy. I am proud to be one of those people.

During his first term in the Senate, Inouye was a strong backer of the Democratic reform agendas of President John F. Kennedy, who was assassinated in 1963, and of Kennedy's successor, President Lyndon B. Johnson. Having personally experienced racial discrimination, Inouye was a particularly enthusiastic supporter of Kennedy's and Johnson's ground-breaking civil rights programs. He was thrilled when Johnson persuaded Congress to approve the sweeping Civil Rights Act of 1964, which outlawed job discrimination against nonwhites and women and authorized the attorney general to guarantee voting rights and end public school segregation, among other things. The only event in 1964 that brought Inouye more satisfaction than the passage of the Civil Rights Act was the birth of his and Margaret's first—and, as it would turn out, only—child, Daniel Ken Inouye, Jr., on July 14.

Inouye was as loyal a champion of Johnson's social welfare—or "Great Society"—program as he was of the Democratic president's far-reaching civil rights legislation. He worked tirelessly to gain support in the Senate for the central components of Johnson's Great Society agenda, including increased aid to education, Medicare and Medicaid to provide quality health care to the elderly and the poor, and a wide-ranging "War on Poverty" in the nation's big cities and rural areas.

In 1965, the same year that Johnson announced the Great Society program, Inouye and his congressional colleagues approved a new act that finally put inhabitants of all nations on an equal footing for immigration to the United States. Japanese immigration to the United States was no longer prohibited after the passage of the Immigration and Nationality Act of 1952. Yet more than a decade later, discriminatory U.S. immigration quotas continued to heavily favor immigrants from western and northern Europe over those from other parts of the world.

According to the Immigration Act of October 3, 1965, prospective immigrants could no longer be excluded on the basis of race, religious creed, or national origin. The act had a dramatic and lasting effect on immigration to the United States: Before the mid-1960s, the large majority of immigrants to the country had been of European origin; since 1965, most have come from Asia, Mexico, or Central and South America.

Johnson overwhelmingly defeated his Republican opponent, Senator Barry Goldwater, in the 1964 presidential election. By 1968, however, Johnson's popularity among the American people had fallen drastically. At the heart of the public dissatisfaction were Johnson's policies in Southeast Asia. In 1954, the small Southeast Asian country of Vietnam had been divided into two separate nations: Communist-controlled North Vietnam and South Vietnam, which had a republican form of government. By the mid-1950s, Viet Cong—Communist guerilla fighters from the North—had begun to sneak into the South. Worried about the spread of Communism in the Far East, President Eisenhower sent U.S. military advisers to South Vietnam to help train its army, a policy that was continued by Eisenhower's successor, John F. Kennedy. Johnson, however, was prepared to do far more to ensure that South Vietnam did not fall to the Communists. Not long after assuming office, he began to beef up the American military presence in Southeast Asia; by 1967, 500,000 U.S. troops were deployed in South Vietnam.

With U.S. casualties mounting and no end to the fighting in sight, by the time of the presidential primaries in 1968, more and more Americans—including many within Johnson's own Democratic Party—had become deeply disillusioned with the war in Vietnam. Inouye, however, remained staunchly loyal to Johnson and his military policies. When the president announced that he would not run for reelection in 1968, Inouye promptly threw his support to Johnson's handpicked successor for the Democratic nomination, Vice President Hubert Humphrey, instead of to the popular antiwar candidate, Senator Eugene McCarthy.

In August 1968, the Democratic National Convention was held in Chicago to choose the party's candidates for president and vice president. Impressed by Inouye's stellar military record and speaking skills, as well as by his unstinting loyalty to party leaders Johnson and Humphrey, convention organizers invited the young senator to give the keynote address to the delegates on August 29, 1968. That year had been a particularly tense year for the nation, marked by violent race riots in several major

DANIEL INOUYE'S KEYNOTE ADDRESS TO THE DEMOCRATIC NATIONAL CONVENTION, AUGUST 29, 1968

The following excerpts are from Daniel Inouye's keynote address to the Democratic National Convention in Chicago, delivered on the evening of August 29, 1968. At that time, the country was reeling from the recent assassinations of Dr. Martin Luther King, Jr., and Senator Robert Kennedy; major race riots in Detroit and other cities; and a rash of Vietnam War protests.

My fellow Americans: This is my country. Many of us have fought hard for the right to say that. . . .

This is our country.

And we are engaged in a time of great testing—testing whether this nation, or any nation conceived in liberty and dedicated to opportunity for all its citizens, can not only endure but continue to progress. The issue before all of us in such a time is how shall we discharge, how shall we honor our citizenship. . . .

Even as we emerge from an era of unsurpassed social and economic progress, Americans are clearly in no mood for counting either their blessings or their bank accounts.

We are still embarked on the longest unbroken journey of economic growth and prosperity in our history. Yet we are cities, the assassinations of civil rights leader Martin Luther King, Jr., and presidential candidate Robert F. Kennedy, and antiwar demonstrations at university campuses across the nation. In his speech, Inouye called for Americans of all ages, races, and religions to pull together during these chaotic times and to take positive action to address the country's problems.

Inouye's stirring words earned widespread acclaim for the relatively unknown senator, and he soon found himself on the

torn by dissension and disrespect for our institutions and leaders is rife across the land. . .

The true dimension of the challenge facing us is a loss of faith. I do not mean simply a loss of religious faith, although this erosion is a major contributor to our unease.

I mean a loss of faith in our country, in its purposes and its institutions. I mean a retreat from the responsibilities of citizenship.

The plain fact is that in the face of complexity and frustration, too many Americans have drifted into the use of power for purely destructive purposes. Too many Americans have come to believe it is their right to decide as individuals which of our laws they will obey and which they will violate.

I do not mean that all our laws are just. They're not and I don't mean to suggest that protest against unjust laws is not proper. Performed in an orderly manner, the right to protest is a cornerstone of our system. . . .

Fellow Americans, this is our country. Its future is what we, its citizens, will make it. And as we all know, we have much to do. Putting aside hatred on the one hand and timidity on the other, let us grow fresh faith in our purpose and new vigor in our citizenship.

short list of vice-presidential candidates for the Democratic nominee, Hubert Humphrey. In the end, Humphrey selected Senator Edmund Muskie of Maine as his running mate. Nonetheless, the national exposure that Inouye's televised speech at the convention brought him only added to his popularity at home: In November 1968, Inouye won reelection to the U.S. Senate with a remarkable 83 percent of the vote. Humphrey was not as successful at the polls that fall: He lost to Republican Richard Nixon by a very slim margin.

Throughout Lyndon Johnson's presidency, Inouye had remained an ardent champion of American military intervention in Vietnam. During the first year and a half of Richard Nixon's presidency, he continued to defend the war, despite growing antiwar sentiment in Congress and throughout the nation. When Nixon assumed the presidency in January 1969, he announced the "Vietnamization" of the war. This policy stated that responsibility for South Vietnam's defense would gradually be transferred from the half-million U.S. troops stationed there to the South Vietnamese army and government. At first, the policy enjoyed widespread popular support. By the end of 1969, however, with nearly 475,000 U.S. troops still deployed in South Vietnam, many Americans were growing impatient with Vietnamization. Adding to the public disillusionment with Nixon's handling of the war was his decision to expand the fighting into Cambodia during the spring of 1970, when U.S. and South Vietnamese forces raided Communist military supply routes and sanctuaries there. During that same spring, Daniel Inouye finally joined other antiwar Democrats in Congress in calling for an immediate end to American military involvement in Vietnam.

The chief reason for Inouye's change of heart regarding the Vietnam War was neither the slow pace of Vietnamization nor Nixon's extension of the war into Cambodia. Rather, it stemmed from the chilling testimony Inouye heard before the Senate Armed Services Committee regarding an incident that came to be known as the My Lai Massacre. On March 16, 1968, a U.S. infantry company entered the village of My Lai in the district of Son My. This area had extensive land mines planted by the Vietcong, probably with the assistance of sympathetic South Vietnamese civilians. Many members of the infantry company had been killed or maimed near My Lai over the past several weeks, and the men were frustrated and bitter. Under the command of Lieutenant William Calley, the soldiers were supposed to be conducting a house-to-house search for Viet Cong. Instead, they rounded up everyone in the village and began to fire at them indiscriminately. Before they were done, they had killed as many as 500 civilians, including many women and children. The American public did not learn of the massacre until late 1969, when the press finally heard of the story. By that time, Calley had already been charged with murder and was awaiting trial by an army tribunal.

In April 1970, the Senate Armed Services Committee began hearings on the My Lai Massacre. For several weeks, Inouye and the other committee members heard eyewitness testimony and reviewed photographs of murdered Vietnamese civilians. Shocked and sickened by what he saw and heard, for the first time, Inouye began to question the fundamental morality of the war. Because he had the least seniority of all the committee members, Inouye was the last senator to ask questions. He had only one question, Inouye said, and that was for his fellow senators: Did the senators think that, if American soldiers had been fighting in Europe rather than in Asia, they would have been as willing to shoot women and children as they had been at My Lai? There was a sudden silence in the room, Inouye later recalled, as the other committee members considered the role that racial prejudice may have played in the atrocities at My Lai.

After the My Lai hearings, Inouye started to support antiwar bills in the Senate. In 1973, the same year that a cease-fire was finally signed between the United States and North Vietnam, he co-sponsored the historic War Powers Act. In direct response to Johnson's and Nixon's aggressive actions in Vietnam and Cambodia, the new act required the president to consult with Congress within 48 hours of any U.S. military operation in a hostile area and withdraw troops within 60 days unless Congress specifically directed otherwise.

In early 1973, a major turning point in Inouye's political career occurred when Senate Majority Leader Mike Mansfield asked him to serve on the Senate Select Committee on Presidential Campaign Activities, better known as the Senate Watergate Committee. Made up of four Democratic and three Republican senators, the committee had been formed to examine allegations that officials in the Nixon administration had committed, or conspired to conceal, illegal actions on behalf of the president's 1972 reelection campaign. "Watergate" was the name of the apartment-office complex in Washington, D.C., where the Democratic National Committee (DNC) headquarters was housed. In June 1972, agents hired by the Committee to Reelect the President to wiretap the DNC's phones were caught breaking into the DNC headquarters. A major focus of the Senate Watergate Committee was whether high-ranking administration officials had authorized the wiretaps and break-in and then plotted to cover up White House involvement in the case.

The televised Watergate Committee hearings won Inouye national attention and respect for his low-key yet probing interrogations of important administration figures, including chief White House aides H.R. Haldeman and John Erlichman. The usually reserved Inouye did commit a blunder at one point during Erlichman's testimony, however: Unaware that his microphone was still on, he muttered, "What a liar!" Erlichman's lawyer, John J. Wilson, retaliated by referring to Inouye as "that little Jap" in front of several reporters. When

Senator Daniel Inouye questions a witness at the hearings of the Senate Select Committee on Presidential Campaign Activities. The bipartisan committee investigated the so-called Watergate Scandal involving high ranking officials in President Richard Nixon's administration. The televised hearings turned the Democratic senator from Hawaii into a national celebrity.

Wilson's racist remark was made public, letters and telegrams poured into the Watergate Committee from Hawaii and all over the mainland in defense of the much-decorated Japanese-American war hero. By the time that the televised hearings ended in February 1974, Inouye's favorable rating among regular viewers stood at nearly 85 percent—the highest mark awarded to any of the seven committee members.

The Watergate investigation eventually resulted in the conviction and imprisonment of several of Nixon's closest aides. On August 9, 1974, after the Judiciary Committee of the House of Representatives voted to recommend the chief executive's impeachment, Nixon became the first U.S. president to resign from the office. The smooth transition of power from Nixon to his successor, former Vice President Gerald Ford, left Inouye with a renewed sense of respect for his nation and its democratic institutions. "When Richard Nixon left Washington," he would later muse, "there were no tanks in our streets, no uniformed men with submachine guns walking patrol. He left, a new person came in, and that was it. . . . That moment made me a very, very proud American."

9

For Hawaii and the Nation

Within six months of Richard Nixon's resignation in August 1974, a new scandal rocked Washington, D.C.: A series of disturbing disclosures concerning misconduct by the CIA, the FBI, and other government intelligence agencies began to appear in the press. Revelations of secret efforts to overthrow elected governments abroad, assassinate foreign leaders, and gather information on the political activities of U.S. citizens shocked many in Congress and the American public. In response to these abuses of power, the Senate quickly established a special investigative panel. One of the panel's chief recommendations was the creation of a permanent Senate committee to devise guidelines for the different intelligence agencies and make sure that they received effective congressional oversight in the future.

In May 1976, the 17-person Senate Select Committee on Intelligence (SSCI) was officially established. For the high-profile position of committee chairman, Senate Majority Leader Robert Byrd chose Daniel Inouye. Byrd reasoned that the World War II hero's unquestioned patriotism combined with his widely acclaimed performance on the Watergate Committee would help win the trust of the American public and the intelligence community alike.

Under Inouye's skillful leadership, the SSCI created a set of detailed rules for covert intelligence operations at home and abroad. The committee also strongly endorsed the Hughes-Ryan Amendment of 1974, which requires the president to explain in writing to the SSCI and its counterpart in the House of Representatives his reasons for authorizing any covert (secret) action. In 1979, after just one term as chairman, Inouye insisted on relinquishing his post. He explained that any chairperson who stayed in the position for more than one term was in danger of developing too cozy a relationship with the intelligence agencies. That could compromise his or her ability to oversee the organizations fairly and effectively. After serving various terms on the SCCI, Inouye left for good in 1994, in accordance with the committee rule that no member may serve for more than eight years.

Inouye's service on the Senate Intelligence Committee and the Watergate Committee, along with his reputation for personal integrity, made him the natural choice to head a Senate panel that was created to investigate yet another major political scandal. This scandal, the so-called Iran-Contra Affair or Irangate, occurred in President Ronald Reagan's second term in office. In early 1987, Inouye was appointed chairman of the Senate Select Committee on Secret Military Assistance to Iran and the Nicaraguan Opposition, which held nationally televised hearings on the scandal from May through August of that year.

At the heart of the Iran-Contra Affair was a secret arrangement engineered by officials in the National Security Council, the president's advisory cabinet for covert operations and security affairs. The arrangement involved two distant nations: Iran, an avowed enemy of the United States, and the Central-American country of Nicaragua. Under the secret arrangement, the NSC officials arranged for the sale of American weapons to Iran. At the time, Iran was involved in a bloody war with its neighbor Iraq. Some of the profits from those sales were then used to help fund the Contras, right-wing guerrilla fighters dedicated to overthrowing Nicaragua's elected socialist government. These actions clearly violated a U.S. trade and arms ban against Iran, as well as recent congressional legislation that forbade any government agency from giving further military aid to the Contra rebels.

Although he was a strong Democrat, Daniel Inouye's chief concern in organizing the new Senate Select Committee was to ensure that the hearings did not turn into a battle between the five members of the Democrat party and five Republican panel members and their respective legal staffs. Hoping to make the hearings as inclusive in character as possible, Inouye insisted that, unlike the Watergate Committee, the new committee would not have separate Republican and Democratic staffs that followed different agendas, interviewed different witnesses, and sometimes failed to share their findings. Even more striking than his commitment to creating a unified, bipartisan support staff was Inouye's decision to name the highest-ranking Republican on the committee, Warren Rudman, as his vice chairman. Rudman was both surprised and moved when, after informing him of his appointment, Inouye assured the senator that he was "going to tell all the Democrats on the committee that as far as I'm concerned, when I'm not there, you will preside."

Inouye's efforts to keep the Select Committee and its investigation above politics won him widespread respect on and off of Capitol Hill. His insistence that the NSC officials and others called before the committee be given wide latitude in answering the panel's questions was not as well received. Critics contended that Inouye's laid-back method of questioning witnesses merely encouraged them to make self-serving speeches rather than testify. Indeed, the nationally broadcast hearings quickly turned

Oliver North prepares to testify before the joint House-Senate Iran–
Contra hearings. The hearings proved to be a showcase for Inouye's
political talents. Concerned with seeking the truth rather than following a
partisan agenda, Inouye upheld the morals and principles that define the
U.S. government.

into a showcase for the attractive and well-spoken Lieutenant
Colonel Oliver North, a former member of the NSC and a key
player in the Iran-Contra Affair. North, a crowd-pleasing ma-
rine, included plenty of personal commentary in his testimony:
He portrayed himself as a defender of patriotism and a good
soldier whose highest duty was to obey his superiors, even if
what they asked him to do was against the law.

In his concluding remarks on August 3, 1987, the final day
of the televised Iran-Contra hearings, Inouye spoke eloquently
of the web of "deceit and duplicity and the arrogant disregard
for the rule of law" that the investigation had uncovered within

the NSC. He was particularly bothered, he said, by North's assertion that survival in a "dangerous world" sometimes called for measures outside of the bounds of the law:

> That, my fellow citizens, is an excuse for autocracy, not policy. . . . Our system of government has withstood the tests and tensions of civil conflict, the Depression and two world wars, times hardly less challenging than our own present.
>
> Indeed, as our greatest military leaders, such as Washington, Marshall, and Eisenhower, have recognized, our form of government is what gives us strength. It must be safeguarded, particularly when times are dangerous and the temptation to arrogate power is the greatest. Vigilance abroad does not require us to abandon our ideas of rule of law at home.
>
> On the contrary, without our principles and without our ideals we have little that is special or worthy to defend.

Almost exactly one year after the Iran-Contra hearings ended, President Reagan signed the groundbreaking Civil Liberties Act of 1988 into law, pledging $20,000 in reparations (damages) to each American resident of Japanese ancestry who was deprived of property and freedom during World War II. Nearly four decades after 120,000 Japanese Americans were forced into desolate internment camps, the U.S. government was at last trying to make amends for this discriminatory wartime policy. On hand to witness the historic signing was Daniel Inouye, one of the chief architects of the movement to finally gain justice for the former internees.

The Civil Liberties Act of 1988 had its roots almost a decade earlier in 1979, when Senator Inouye proposed that Congress create a special commission to study the detainment of ethnic

Japanese residents of the Pacific Coast between 1941 and 1945 and report its conclusions to Congress. The following year, Congress acted on Inouye's suggestion by forming the Commission on Wartime Relocation and Internment of Civilians (CWRIC). The Japanese-American community overwhelmingly supported the new congressional investigation: Since World War II, community leaders had been calling on the U.S. government to apologize for its actions and provide some form of monetary compensation to the internees, many of whom had lost their homes, businesses, and many of their personal possessions.

"A LEGACY OF HONOR AND PRIDE"

Daniel Inouye has maintained close ties with his fellow veterans of the 442nd Regimental Combat Team over the decades. In 1993, hundreds of former members of the "Go for Broke" regiment met in Honolulu to celebrate the fiftieth anniversary of the creation of their all–Japanese-American unit. Senator Inouye was invited to give the keynote address at the reunion. It is excerpted below.

Over the years, many have asked us—"Why?" "Why did you fight and serve so well?" My son, like your sons and daughters, has asked the same question—"Why?" "Why were you willing and ready to give your life?". . .

I told my son it was a matter of honor. I told him about my father's farewell message when I left home to put on the uniform of my country. My father was not a man of eloquence but he said, "Whatever you do, do not dishonor the family and do not dishonor the country." I told my son that for many of us, to have done any less than what we had done in battle would have dishonored our families and our country.

Second, I told my son that there is an often-used Japanese phrase—*Kodomo no tame ni*. Though most of us who went into battle were young and single, we wanted to leave a

Over a period of more than two years, the CWRIC compiled thousands of pages of evidence from military and government documents and held hearings in nearly a dozen American cities at which former internees testified about their wartime experiences. In 1983, the commission published its findings: The relocation and internment had not been justified by military necessity as the Roosevelt administration claimed. The report insisted that the real reasons for the government's internment policy were racial prejudice and wartime hysteria. The commission recommended that the U.S. government extend a

legacy of honor and pride and the promise of a good life for our yet-to-be-born children and their children.

My brothers, I believe we can assure ourselves that we did succeed in upholding our honor and that of our families and our nation. And I respectfully and humbly believe that our service and the sacrifices of those who gave their all on the battlefield assure a better life for our children and their children.

Yes, I believe we can stand tall this evening in knowing that our journey together, a journey that began on that tragic Sunday morning, was not in vain. And so tonight, let us embrace with our hearts and minds the memory of those brothers who are not with us this evening and let us do so with all of our affection and gratitude. Let us embrace with deep love our loved ones for having stood with us and walked with us on our journey. Let us embrace with everlasting gratitude and Aloha the many friends and neighbors who supported us throughout our journey. Let us embrace with everlasting love our great nation.

And finally, let us embrace our sons and daughters with full pride and with the restful assurance that the story of our journey of honor will live on for generations to come.

formal apology to the surviving internees, along with monetary reparations. In large measure thanks to the dedication and determination of Daniel Inouye and fellow Japanese American congressmen Spark Matsunaga, Robert Matsui, and Norman Mineta, these recommendations became law on August 10, 1988, when President Reagan signed the Civil Liberties Act. Under the provisions of the act, more than 82,000 individuals would eventually receive reparation payments of $20,000 each. The act also authorized $50 million to fund education and research about the Japanese-American internment in order to help ensure that such an injustice would not occur in the United States again.

In the years since he chaired the Senate Select Committee on Secret Military Assistance to Iran and the Nicaraguan Opposition in 1987, Daniel Inouye has served with distinction as a chair, co-chair, and ranking minority member on a variety of influential Senate committees. These bodies include the Committee on Commerce, Science, and Transportation; the Committee on Rules and Administration; the Appropriations Committee; and the Committee on Indian Affairs.

Author Deborah Gillan Straub noted that, from his first years in Congress in the early 1960s, Inouye "has tended to have a liberal opinion on social issues but a more moderate or even conservative view on . . . defense issues." The Democratic senator's liberal stance on social issues has been reflected in his generally consistent support for social welfare and environmental protection programs, consumer protection laws, gun control, and abortion rights. His more conservative stance on defense-related matters is evident in his long service as the chairman or ranking minority member of the Defense Subcommittee of the Senate Appropriations Committee. During Republican and Democratic administrations alike, Inouye has frequently championed substantial increases in military appropriations, especially for the development of new and technologically advanced weaponry such as the neutron bomb.

Inouye's struggle with racial discrimination during and immediately after World War II sparked his interest in serving on another high-profile Senate committee, the Committee on Indian Affairs, which he chaired from 1987 to 1995 and 2001 to 2003. During his tenure on the committee, Inouye has consistently championed the rights of American Indian, native Alaskan, and native Hawaiian peoples. He has sponsored or cosponsored a variety of bills that address their unique challenges and needs in areas such as education, health care, and economic development. A strong supporter of the American Indian and Alaska native governments, Inouye strongly believes that native Hawaiians should be allowed to form a similar governing body. In 2000, Daniel Akaka, Inouye's fellow Democratic senator from Hawaii and a native Hawaiian himself, first introduced the Native Hawaiian Government Reorganization Act to Congress. Since then, Inouye has been a loyal backer of the measure. Although passed by the House of Representatives, the bill has been stalled in the Senate for years, mostly because of concerns by some conservative Republicans that it would create an unconstitutional, race-based government.

Throughout his more than four decades in Congress, Inouye has dedicated himself to serving the interests of his state's people. He has pushed for affordable housing, better health care and educational opportunities for Hawaii's children, jobs for its economy, and federal protection for the Islands' natural resources. As a member of the Senate Appropriations Committee, Inouye has steered billions of dollars in federal money to his state over the years, including nearly $500 million in defense funds in 2005 alone.

Inouye is particularly proud of his part in helping secure the return of the island of Kahoolawe to his home state. Kahoolawe, the smallest island in the Hawaiian archipelago, had been used by the U.S. military for target practice since the 1920s. After the attack on Pearl Harbor, the navy took full control of it and

Republican Colorado Senator Ben Nighthorse Campbell, left, and Senator Daniel Inouye view a groundbreaking ceremony for the National Museum of the American Indian on September 28, 1999, in Washington, D.C. Tribal leaders from across the country gathered to celebrate the groundbreaking for the $110 million museum on the National Mall.

the island's residents were ordered to leave. The island quickly became covered with craters because it was used extensively by the navy for bombing and gunnery training. Since the end of World War II, Islanders had been fighting to halt the bombing and bring Kahoolawe back under Hawaiian control. Owing in large measure to the persistent efforts of Inouye and his congressional colleagues from Hawaii, the long campaign was finally won in 1993: The U.S. government agreed to hand back Kahoolawe to the Hawaiian people and approved a nearly $500 million clean up fund for the island.

Inouye's success in securing large sums of federal money for Hawaii has made him a favorite target of Citizens Against Government Waste, a nonpartisan "pork-barrel" watchdog group. In 2001 and again in 2005, the group awarded Inouye their "Porker of the Month" award for what they considered reckless wasting of federal taxpayer dollars on projects designed to benefit people in his home district. Inouye believes that the group's criticism of him is unjust: "The report by the Citizens Against Government Waste suggests very clearly to me that I am doing the job I was elected to do by the people of Hawaii," Inouye told reporter Debbie Sokei after receiving his first "Porker of the Month" award in March 2001. "Anyone who studies the projects that I supported should conclude that they are important and necessary. These are all good projects. Moreover, many of these projects, such as the environmental, health, education and defense initiatives, have a positive effect on the nation as a whole."

10

Into the Twenty-first Century

On June 21, 2000, more than half a century after his heroic actions at Colle Musatello near San Terenzo, Italy, Daniel Inouye was finally granted his country's highest military award, the Congressional Medal of Honor. During a moving White House ceremony, President Bill Clinton awarded Inouye and 21 other Japanese Americans Medals of Honor for their outstanding valor during World War II. The awards followed a special congressional reevaluation of the combat records of Asian Americans who had received the military's second-highest honor, the Distinguished Cross, during the war. Before 2000, just one American of Japanese descent had been granted the Medal of Honor for military service during World War II. This injustice irritated many within and outside the Japanese American community and prompted Inouye's colleague from Hawaii, Senator Daniel Akaka, to sponsor the bill that led to the congressional review. "Senator Inouye, you wrote that your father told you as you left at age 18 to join the Army and fight a war that the Inouyes owe

President Bill Clinton presents the prestigious Medal of Honor to Senator Daniel Inouye on June 21, 2000, at the White House. Twenty-one other Japanese Americans were also awarded Medals of Honor that day for exhibiting bravery during World War II.

an unrepayable debt to America," President Clinton said during the White House ceremony. "If I may say so, sir, more than half a century later, America owes an unrepayable debt to you and your colleagues."

Inouye's wartime experiences have given him enormous respect for the men and women who serve in the U.S. military. At the same time, it has made him extremely wary of sending

JAPANESE AMERICAN POLITICAL FIGURES FROM HAWAII

Daniel Inouye became the first Japanese American to be elected to the U.S. House of Representatives in 1959 and the U.S. Senate in 1962, and his success on the national political scene set an important precedent for other Hawaiians of Japanese descent. Two influential and highly respected Japanese-American politicians from Hawaii who followed Inouye to Congress during the early 1960s were Spark M. Matsunaga and Patsy Takemoto Mink.

Spark Masayuki Matsunaga was born to Issei parents on the Hawaiian Island of Kauai in 1916. An outstanding student, he graduated from the University of Hawaii just six months before the Japanese attack on Pearl Harbor. Like Inouye, when the United States entered World War II in December 1941, Matsunaga wanted nothing more than to fight for his country. In 1943, he finally got his chance when the all-Nisei 442nd Regimental Combat Team was formed. Wounded twice in battle, Matsunaga was awarded a Purple Heart for bravery under fire and promoted to the rank of captain before being honorably discharged in 1945. After graduating from Harvard Law School in 1951, Matsunaga became active in the territory's Democratic Party, like many other Nisei veterans in Hawaii.

After serving in the territorial legislature for seven years, Matsunaga was elected to the new state Senate in 1959. In 1962, he moved to the national stage, winning Inouye's former seat in the U.S. House of Representatives the same year that his old friend from the 442nd was elected to the U.S. Senate for the first time. He was reelected to the House five times, and, in 1976, Matsunaga defeated his Republican opponent to join Inouye in the Senate.

For the next 14 years, until his death in 1990, Matsunaga served as the junior senator from Hawaii. During the 1980s, he worked closely with Inouye to gain monetary compensation for the more than 100,000 American residents of Japanese descent who were sent to internment camps during World War II. World peace, however, remained the Nisei veteran's main concern throughout his tenure in Congress. As one of the government's most ardent supporters of arms control, Matsunaga also helped push legislation through Congress to create the United States Institute of Peace, which promotes nonviolent resolutions to international conflicts.

Arguably the most famous Asian-American woman in Hawaiian history, Patsy Takemoto Mink was born on Maui in 1927 to Japanese immigrant parents. A woman ahead of her time, Patsy graduated from the University of Hawaii in 1948 and the University of Chicago Law School in 1953. While in Chicago, she met and married John Mink. After moving back to Hawaii in the mid-1950s, Patsy Mink became the first Japanese-American woman in Hawaii to practice law and started to volunteer for the Democratic Party. Always a groundbreaker, in 1956, she became the first Asian-American woman to be elected to the territorial legislature. She lost to Daniel Inouye in the special election for Hawaii's seat in the U.S. House of Representatives in 1959 but was elected to the Hawaiian State Senate in 1962. Two years later, when Hawaii was awarded a second representative in the House of Representatives, Senator Inouye backed Mink's successful bid for the new seat. In January 1965, she became the first Asian-American woman to serve in Congress.

During the 1960s and 1970s, Congresswoman Mink was a strong supporter of civil rights, child welfare programs, and education. During the early 1970s, she was a prime backer of Title IX, which outlawed gender discrimination at any educational institution that received federal funds. An outspoken opponent of the Vietnam War, Mink blasted the costly conflict for taking money away from programs designed to help the nation's underprivileged. In 1972, she gained national attention when she made a bid for the Democratic presidential nomination, running on an antiwar and pro–women's rights platform.

Mink ran unsuccessfully in the Democratic primary for senator against Spark Matsunaga in 1976. After the loss, she once again

(continues)

(*continued*)

became a private attorney in Honolulu. A little more than a decade later, Senator Matsunaga's untimely death prompted Mink to return to politics. In 1990, after Congressman Daniel Akaka was appointed to succeed Matsunaga in the Senate, Mink won a special election for Akaka's vacant House seat. Reelected in 2000, she focused much of her attention on women's issues and became a firm supporter of universal health care. After a bout with pneumonia, Patsy Takemoto Mink died in September 2002, at the age of 74.

American soldiers off to war unnecessarily. "I learned on the battlefield that war is not about glory. It is about suffering and death. As a U.S. Senator, I have tried my best to prevent and avoid war," he declared in an interview published in the journal *The Officer* in 2000. In late 1990, President George H.W. Bush was preparing to take military action against Iraq in what came to be known as the Persian Gulf War. Inouye was one of a handful of congressmen who urged restraint in responding to Iraq's invasion of neighboring Kuwait.

A little more than a decade later, in the fall of 2002, Congress debated whether to authorize President George W. Bush to use military force to resolve a new dispute with Iraq and its leader, Saddam Hussein. Inouye again expressed doubts regarding the necessity and wisdom of his president's war policy. He believed that the president had failed to provide credible evidence that Iraq posed an immediate threat to national security or that Saddam possessed—or was close to developing—weapons of mass destruction, as the Bush administration insisted. Consequently, Inouye was deeply concerned about how he could justify a preemptive attack on Iraq to his constituents whose husbands, wives, sons, and daughters would be ordered into battle. "I've

Daniel Inouye speaks during the 63rd annual commemoration of the bombing of Pearl Harbor on December 7, 2004, in Pearl Harbor, Hawaii. With U.S. troops fighting in Iraq and Afghanistan, Americans marked the anniversary of the Japanese attack on Pearl Harbor with a salute to the nation's resilience 63 years earlier.

got to be able to tell them why," Inouye declared. "I want to support the president, but I want to make certain my support is not misplaced." In the end, Inouye became one of just 23 senators to vote against the War Powers Resolution of October 2002, which authorized the United States to attack Iraq if Saddam refused to give up his alleged weapons of mass destruction— weapons that were never found after the U.S. invasion of Iraq in March 2003.

In November 2004, Daniel Inouye was elected to his eighth term as senator from Hawaii. By then, the 80-year-old statesman had become the fourth-longest-serving senator in American history. As of 2006, only two of his colleagues in the Senate had more seniority: Robert Byrd of West Virginia and Edward Kennedy of Massachusetts. Inouye has no plans to retire any time in the near future. "There's still work to be done," he recently told a reporter, "I can't think of anyone saying, 'I've done everything I wanted to do and I've finished it.'"

CHRONOLOGY

1898 Hawaii is annexed by the United States as a territory.

1899 Daniel Inouye's grandparents and father come to Hawaii from Yokoyama, Japan.

1924 Daniel Inouye is born to Hyotaro and Kame Inouye in Honolulu on September 7; Congress bans all new Japanese immigration to the United States.

1941 Japan attacks Pearl Harbor, Hawaii, on December 7, and the United States enters World War II.

1942 Daniel graduates from McKinley High School in Honolulu.

1943 Inouye is accepted into the all–Japanese-American 442nd Regimental Combat Team.

1945 Inouye is severely wounded in Italy a few weeks before Germany surrenders to the Allies in May; Japan surrenders soon after atomic bombs devastate Hiroshima and Nagasaki in August.

1948 Inouye marries Margaret Shinobu Awamura on June 12.

1950 Inouye graduates from the University of Hawaii with a degree in government and economics.

1952 He graduates from George Washington University Law School; Congress finally allows immigrants from Japan (the Issei) to become U.S. citizens.

1953–1954 Inouye serves as deputy public prosecutor of the City and County of Honolulu.

1954 He is elected to Hawaii's territorial House of Representatives and is reelected in 1956.

1958 Inouye is elected to the territorial Senate.

1959 Inouye is elected to U.S. House of Representatives as first representative of the new state of Hawaii.

1962 He becomes the first Japanese American to be elected to the U.S. Senate.

1964 Daniel Ken Inouye, Jr., is born to Daniel and Margaret Inouye on July 14.

1968 Inouye delivers the keynote address to the Democratic National Convention.

1973–1974 Inouye serves on the Senate Watergate Committee.

TIMELINE

1945
Inouye is severely wounded in Italy a few weeks before the end of World War II in Europe.

1924
Daniel Inouye is born to Hyotaro and Kame Inouye in Honolulu on September 7.

1899

1954

1899
Daniel Inouye's grandparents and father come to Hawaii from Japan.

1954
He is elected to Hawaii's territorial House of Representatives.

1941
Japan attacks Pearl Harbor, Hawaii, on December 7, and the United States enters World War II.

1976–1979 He serves as the first chairman of the Senate Select Committee on Intelligence.

1987 Inouye chairs the Senate panel to examine the Iran-Contra Affair.

2000 Inouye is awarded the Medal of Honor in June for his World War II service, along with 19 other Nisei veterans.

2004 Inouye is elected to his eighth term as U.S. Senator from Hawaii.

1959
Inouye is elected to U.S. House of Representatives as first representative of the new state of Hawaii.

1973–1974
Inouye serves on the Senate Watergate Committee.

2004
Inouye is elected to his eighth term as a U.S. Senator from Hawaii.

1959

2004

1987
Inouye chairs the Senate panel to examine the Iran-Contra Affair.

1962
He becomes the first Japanese American to be elected to the U.S. Senate.

2000
Inouye is awarded the Medal of Honor in June for World War II service, along with 19 other Nisei veterans.

GLOSSARY

archipelago—An island group.

aliens—Individuals who are not citizens of the country in which they live.

Buddhism—One of the major religions of Japan, whose central principle is that life is suffering, which can be escaped by renouncing all worldly desires and following the Eightfold Path of right faith, meditation, judgment, actions, obedience, language, livelihood, and memory.

dekaseginin—A term used to refer to Japanese workers who intended to return to their homeland after working in the United States or its territories for several years.

furo—A traditional Japanese-style bathtub.

haole—The Hawaiian term for Caucasians.

internment—The forced removal and confinement of people during wartime.

Issei—The Japanese term for "first generation." Most Issei came to the United States and its territories from Japan between 1885 and 1924. Congress finally passed a law. that permitted them to apply for U.S. citizenship in 1952.

luna—The overseer on a Hawaiian sugar plantation.

martial law—The temporary rule of a civilian population by military authorities during a time of emergency.

naturalization—The process of becoming a citizen of a foreign country.

Nisei—The Japanese term for "second generation." The Nisei were the children of the Issei, who were born in the United States and its territories. Unlike their parents, they were American citizens.

on—The Japanese term for duty or obligation.

pidgin English—The Hawaiian dialect that developed during the late nineteenth and early twentieth centuries from a mixture of the various languages of the island chain's main ethnic groups.

Sansei—The Japanese term for "third generation," the children of the Nisei.

Shinto—The native religion of Japan that emphasizes ancestor worship and nature.

tofu—A traditional Japanese food made from soybeans.

Yonsei—The Japanese term for "fourth generation," the children of the Sansei.

BIBLIOGRAPHY

BOOKS

Brokaw, Tom. *The Greatest Generation*. New York: Random House, 1998.

Daws, Gavan. *Shoal of Time: A History of the Hawaiian Islands*. Honolulu: University of Hawaii Press, 1968.

Dole, Bob. *One Soldier's Story: A Memoir*. New York: Harper Collins, 2005.

Fuchs, Lawrence H. *Hawaii Pono: A Social History*. New York: Harcourt, Brace & World, 1961.

Inouye, Daniel K., with Lawrence Elliott. *Journey to Washington*. Englewood Cliffs, NJ: Prentice-Hall, 1967.

Joesting, Edward. *Hawaii: An Uncommon History*. New York: W.W. Norton, 1972.

Johnson, Haynes. *Sleepwalking Through History: America in the Reagan Years*. New York: W.W. Norton, 1991.

Niiya, Brian, ed. *Encyclopedia of Japanese American History*. New York: Facts on File, 2001.

Okihiro, Gary. *Whispered Silences: Japanese Americans and World War II*. Seattle, Wash.: University of Washington Press, 1996.

Smith, Larry. *Beyond Glory: Medal of Honor Heroes in Their Own Words*. New York: W.W. Norton, 2003.

Straub, Deborah Gillan, ed. *Asian American Voices*. New York: UXL, 1997.

Takaki, Ronald. *A Different Mirror: A History of Multicultural America*. Boston: Little, Brown, 1993.

Takaki, Ronald. *Double Victory: A Multicultural History of America in World War II*. Boston: Little, Brown, 2000.

Takaki, Ronald. *Strangers From a Different Shore: A History of Asian Americans*. Boston: Little, Brown, 1989.

Thompson, Fred D. *At That Point in Time: The Inside Story of the Senate Watergate Committee*. New York: Quadrangle, 1975.

Wels, Susan. *December 7, 1941: Pearl Harbor, America's Darkest Day*. San Diego, Calif: Tehabi Books, 2001.

ARTICLES

"Asian American Vets Honored for Service," *USA Today* (June 22, 2000).

Borreca, Richard. "Senator Gives All For State, Nation." *Honolulu Star-Bulletin* (September 16, 1999).

DePledge, Derrick. "Hawaii Delegates Urge Caution Against Iraq." *Honolulu Advertiser* (September 16, 2002).

Pichaske, Pete. "The Bungled Burglary Made Inouye a 'Star': The Hearings Made the Second-Term Senator from Hawaii a National Figure." *Honolulu Star* (June 17, 1997).

Rees, Robert M. "Few Could Take the Place of Inouye." *Honolulu Advertiser* (April 17, 2005).

Reyes, B. J. "At 80, Inouye Still Mindful of Work Ahead of Him." *Honolulu Advertiser* (September 7, 2004).

————. "Senator Daniel K. Inouye Interview." *The Officer* 76 (December 2000): p. 24.

Sokei, Debbie. "Inouye Defends 'Porker of the Month' Title." *Pacific Business News* 39 (March 30, 2001).

Wilborn, Thomas. "World War II: Destiny Unites Disabled Veterans." *DAV Magazine* 46 (March–April 2004): pp. 18–20.

Wright, Walter, "Unit Hails Inouye as Heroes' Hero." *Honolulu Advertiser,* April 7, 2003.

FILMS

Perry, Paul, and Heather Haunani Giugni. *Daniel K. Inouye: An American Story.* Digital Videodisc. Honolulu: Juniroa Productions, 2003.

WEB SITES

"Daniel K. Inouye." Medal of Honor: The Bravest of the Brave. Available online. URL: http://www.medalofhonor.com/DanielInouye.htm.

Nakaso, Dan. "The Japanese American Story: A Testing of Loyalty: December 7, 1941–2001." The Honolulu Advertiser: Pearl Harbor Plus Sixty Years. Available online. URL: http://the.honoluluadvertiser.com/specials/pearlharbor60/chapter4.html.

Official Web Site for Senator Daniel K. Inouye. http://www.senate.gov/~inouye/.

FURTHER READING

BOOKS

Cooper, Michael L. *Fighting for Honor: Japanese Americans and World War II*. New York: Clarion Books, 2000.

Ingram, W. Scott. *Japanese Immigrants*. New York: Facts on File, 2005.

Inouye, Daniel K., with Lawrence Elliott. *Journey to Washington*. Englewood Cliffs, NJ: Prentice-Hall, 1967.

Mattern, Joanne. *Japanese Americans*. Philadelphia: Chelsea House, 2003.

McGowen, Tom. *"Go for Broke": Japanese Americans in World War II*. New York: Franklin Watts, 1995.

Niiya, Brian, ed. *Encyclopedia of Japanese American History*. New York: Facts on File, 2001.

Stein, R. Conrad. *Nisei Regiment*. Chicago: Children's Press, 1985.

Takaki, Ronald. *Issei and Nisei: The Settling of Japanese America*. New York: Chelsea House, 1994.

Zurlo, Tony. *The Japanese Americans*. San Diego, Calif.: Lucent Books, 2003.

WEB SITES

Daniel K. Inouye (Democrat-Hawaii). www.congress.org/congressorg/bio/?id=201

Go For Broke: The History of the 442nd Regimental Combat Team and 100th Infantry Battalion. www.goforbroke.org/history/history.asp

Medal of Honor: The Bravest of the Brave: Daniel K. Inouye Biography. www.medalofhonor.com/DanielInouye.htm

Official Web Site for Senator Daniel K. Inouye. www.senate.gov/~inouye/

PHOTO CREDITS

INDEX

ABOUT
THE AUTHOR

LOUISE CHIPLEY SLAVICEK received her master's degree in history from the University of Connecticut. She is the author of more than a dozen other books for young people, including *Women of the American Revolution*, *Israel*, and *The Great Wall of China*. She lives in Ohio with her husband, Jim, a research biologist, and their two children, Krista and Nathan.